FINANCING YOUR BUSINESS:
Get a Grip on Finding the Money

D1568193

numbers
101 for
SMALL BUSINESS

FINANCING YOUR BUSINESS:
Get a Grip on Finding the Money

Angie Mohr, CA, CMA

REMOVED FROM COLLECTION

3?? ????

Self-Counsel Press
(a division of)
International Self-Counsel Press Ltd.
USA   Canada

WEST ISLIP PUBLIC LIBRARY
3 HIGBIE LANE
WEST ISLIP, NEW YORK 11795

Copyright © 2005 by International Self-Counsel Press Ltd.

All rights reserved.

No part of this book may be reproduced or transmitted in any form by any means — graphic, electronic, or me-chanical — without permission in writing from the publisher, except by a reviewer who may quote brief passages in a review.

Self-Counsel Press acknowledges the financial support of the Government of Canada through the Book Publishing Industry Development Program (BPIDP) for our publishing activities.

Printed in Canada.

First edition: 2005

Library and Archives Canada Cataloguing in Publication

Mohr, Angie
   Financing your business: get a grip on finding the money/Angie Mohr.

(Business series)
ISBN 1-55180-583-9

1. New business enterprises—Finance. 2. Small business—Finance.
I. Title. II. Series: Self-counsel business series.

HG4027.7M633 2004   658.15'22   C2004-904043-X

Self-Counsel Press
(a division of)
International Self-Counsel Press Ltd.

1704 N. State Street	1481 Charlotte Road
Bellingham, WA 98225	North Vancouver, BC V7J 1H1
USA	Canada

Contents

Appendix 1

Appendix 2

Appendix 3

Appendix 4

Glossary

Samples

Tables

Worksheets

Notice to Readers

Laws are constantly changing. Every effort is made to keep this publication as current as possible. However, the author, the publisher, and the vendor of this book make no representation or warranties regarding the outcome or the use to which the information in this book is put and are not assuming any liability for any claims, losses, or damages arising out of the use of this book. The reader should not rely on the author or the publisher of this book for any professional advice. Please be sure that you have the most recent edition.

Acknowledgments

I would like to thank the following people for their assistance and support during the writing of this book:

- Everyone at Self-Counsel Press who has provided guidance and encouragement throughout this project.

- Sam Hiyate, Ellen Roseman, Dave Chilton, and Dave Trahair for all their advice and encouragement.

- All of my accounting and workshop clients who have helped with the direction of the series.

- Friends and family, in particular, my husband, Jeff, and Alex and Erika.

Thanks also to Matt Osborne, one of the finest musicians/small-business owners/human beings I have had the honor of knowing. I will miss you greatly.

Introduction

A Look at Entrepreneurs and Why They Start Businesses

Starting a small business is a dream of many who want to build on their skills and abilities to provide a stable income for themselves and their families, while building a business that will outlive them.

There are as many reasons for starting a business as there are entrepreneurs. For some, it's all about the money. For others, it's security and stability that are most important. Many entrepreneurs find satisfaction and fulfillment in building something from nothing and witnessing the quickening: that point where the business takes on a life of its own.

The freedom that comes from running your own business and being responsible for your own successes (and failures!) is an irresistible pull for most entrepreneurs. It's what fuels them and keeps them going even when money is tight and business is bad. This entrepreneurial drive is what sets business owners apart, what makes them a special breed of individuals.

It is not easy to start a small business, however. It's incredibly hard work that requires great commitment with very little financial reward in the beginning. In many ways, it's a leap of faith, not only for you but for your family and your investors and lenders as well. You will all have to come together to give birth to this new enterprise, with the help of your midwives: your lawyer, accountant, financial planner, and directors.

There are many issues that you will have to weigh and consider, from what type of business you should start to how you are going to operate it to hiring employees. One of the most difficult tasks for the new entrepreneur is finding money. It takes capital to start even the smallest of businesses, and lenders are cautious, if not downright wary, of shelling out money based on an unproven idea.

Your search for financing can be made easier, however, when you follow the basic steps of capital management and plan your business properly from the beginning. Financing is an issue that you will have to deal with not only when you start your business, but continually as your business grows and thrives. New sources of financing will open themselves to you as your business gains a solid financial track record, and you will eventually (even though it may seem difficult to believe in the beginning) have to decide amongst the various offers of capital.

Financing Your Business: Get a Grip on Finding the Money is the fourth book in the *Numbers 101 for Small Business* series, aimed at small-business owners. In it, we will answer many of the questions that you will have as you plan, start, and grow your business, including —

- What kind of business should I start?
- Should I buy an existing business or start one from scratch?
- What is this "business plan" everyone keeps talking about?
- Where am I going to find the money to start up my business?
- How do I find my external advisers?
- How will I know how I stack up against my competition?
- How do I know when it's time to hire people?
- Should I invest in new equipment?
- Where do I get the money to expand my operation?

These questions and many more will be answered in this book as you navigate through your business start-up and growth phases.

How to Use This Book

Financing Your Business walks you through the first steps of planning for your new business. You don't need to read the chapters in sequence. Feel free to browse the table of contents and start with those chapters that interest you or most directly apply to your business. I do, however, recommend that you eventually read the entire book, as each chapter has critical information to help your business. You may find that you will return to some chapters after you have been in business for a while, finding new meaning in them. Return here often to refresh your knowledge of business decision making and the process of seeking financing.

Financing Your Business is applicable regardless of the country or business climate in which you operate. It is not written with specific tax laws or accounting rules in mind. Terminology may differ from country to country, and the dollar signs for some readers might be pounds or rupees or lire for others, but the underlying principles of the book are universally applicable.

We start by looking at the pros and cons of different types of businesses and address which type of business you should start. We then discuss the two main forms of starting a business: buying an existing business and building one from scratch, and how to calculate the comparative financial benefits of each. Chapters 6 through 8 discuss financing: how much you'll need and where it will come from. Chapters 9 through 15 look at specific topics that you will face as you start up your business. Chapter 16 looks at expanding your business: the decision process and finding the money.

Financing Your Business is written in an easy-to-digest manner that caters to busy entrepreneurs. It contains a blend of instruction and illustrated examples of business situations most commonly faced by entrepreneurs.

The information in *Financing Your Business* has been honed from the entrepreneurial workshops, radio broadcasts, and one-to-one training sessions that I have developed in my accounting firm over the years.

There are many downloadable tools and other useful information for small-business owners at <www.numbers101.com>. Please surf by and download templates, screen savers, and other cool tools — and sign up for our free newsletter while you're there.

Financing Your Business is the fourth book in the *Numbers 101 for Small Business* series. If you want to brush up on your accounting basics, you may wish to read *Bookkeepers' Boot Camp,* the first book in the series. It covers the essentials of record keeping for small business and why it's necessary to track information. *Bookkeepers' Boot Camp* also teaches you how to sort through the masses of information and paperwork in your business, how to record what's important for your business, and how to use that information to grow your business for success. If you need help with understanding what your financial statements are trying to tell you, you may wish to pick up *Financial Management 101,* the second book in the series. Here you will find clear, down-to-earth guidance to help you understand how to interpret your business's financial statements and how to use this information to create a more successful business. *Managing Business Growth,* the third book in the *Numbers 101 for Small Business* series, walks you through the process of building a better business, one that runs efficiently and profitably. It looks at those critical processes that separate successful businesses from failures, and how to apply those financial processes to your business.

So, if you're ready to get started, grab a coffee and bring this book, your calculator, and your business ideas to the table. I wish you all the success in the world in starting down the entrepreneurial path. I love to hear from small businesses, so feel free to drop me a line at <angie@numbers101.com> and let me know how you're doing!

So, What Kind of Business Should You Start?

Just because you are a hairdresser doesn't mean you should start a salon. We examine the pros and cons of different types of businesses.

Introduction

Starting a business can be scary, exciting, and fulfilling, all at the same time. Frequently, small businesses are started by people who have been employees in the same industry. For example, hair stylists often open salons and accountants start accounting firms. You may feel that because the industry you've previously worked in is familiar to you, you would be successful at starting a business in this industry.

It's important to keep in mind, however, that building a business, managing a business, and doing what the business does are three very different activities requiring different skill sets. You may be interested in doing only one of these three things. For example, you may get great pleasure out of hair styling, but have little patience for managing the day-to-day operations of a business. In this case, you will want to reconsider your decision to start a business. No matter how much joy it gives you to "be your own boss" while doing the thing that you do best, you will come to despise all the other tasks that go along with owning and managing a small business. On the other hand, you may love building the business: designing the office space, putting together the marketing plan, forecasting, and building the customer base. You may, however, be thoroughly bored with the management aspect or with doing what the business does. Entrepreneurs who feel this way tend to build a business, get it up and running, sell it, and start all over again. The thrill for them is in the creation process.

If you plan to build your business, manage it, and be its chief employee, make sure that you have the energy and the skills to do all three of those things. If not, you will have to hire other people in those positions that you do not wish to do yourself, or rethink your business plan entirely.

Once you have assessed your strengths and weaknesses in terms of building, managing, and operating a business, it's time to look at your personal goals.

Why Do You Want to Be an Entrepreneur?

Before you jump with both feet into starting a business, take some time to examine your motivations. What is it that is driving you towards starting and running a business? Many small-business owners cite things such as more money, freedom, and empire building as their motivators.

Money

Owning and running a business has the potential for providing you with a higher level of investment return and remuneration than you would receive working for someone else. The profit potential is definitely there, but high profits are a trade-off for high risks. Starting a small business is a risky proposition and you, as the owner, face the potential for financial loss as well as gain. It's important to keep this in mind as you build your business and make sure that you not only have the ability to survive failure, but also the ability to tolerate risk. We will examine business risk in greater detail in Chapter 9.

When small-business owners talk about money, though, they often don't mean that they want money for money's sake. Money means something slightly different to each person, but in general, it represents financial independence, prosperity, and security. The more time you spend planning your business model before you begin, the more likely you will be building a profitable enterprise that will meet your personal financial goals.

Freedom

Many small-business owners like the freedom that comes with not having a boss and being able to make their own decisions. However, with this freedom comes ultimate responsibility for the business, including responsibility for customer satisfaction, working conditions, supplier shortages, product failure, and the economic well-being of your employees. Look at whether you are the type of person who can handle these responsibilities while simultaneously making considered, but quick, decisions on a daily basis.

Empire building

For many small-business owners, the most important consideration is that they are building something that will outlive them and perhaps provide income and stability to future generations. If this is an important consideration to you, it will be critical to make sure that you are building a business that has value, and that the value can be transferred to others through sale of the business or inheritance. The unfortunate reality is that over 80 percent of small businesses do not survive into the next generation but die with their owners.

What Kind of Business Should I Start?

The three major types of businesses are manufacturing, retail/wholesale, and service. There are pros and cons to running each type of business, as well as financial considerations. Let's have a look at the characteristics of each one.

Manufacturing business

Manufacturing involves purchasing raw materials and adding labor and specialized machinery to create a product to be sold to customers. An example is a furniture manufacturer. This type of business would buy lumber from a sawmill, as well as nails, screws, glue, and varnish from a supplier. It would then have its employees use saws, drills, and other tools to turn the lumber into tables, chairs, and other furniture.

A manufacturing environment usually requires a hefty upfront investment in the equipment that will be used in the manufacturing process. Manufacturers also tend to need more highly skilled workers than, for example, a retail business. For these reasons, it is very difficult to start up a manufacturing business on a small scale and expand as you go along.

One of the main benefits of this type of business is that it can service very large customers with very specialized products. For example, a manufacturer can supply the entire North American auto industry with injection-molded fan vents.

Retail/Wholesale business

Retailing and wholesaling involves the purchase and resale of products. A retailer sells the products to the final consumer while the wholesaler is simply an intermediary, selling the product to another business that will ultimately sell it to the final consumer.

Almost every store that you can think of is a retailer. For example, a bookstore will purchase books from the publisher and display them for sale in the store. An example of a wholesaler is an importer that purchases teapots from Japan and sells them to stores, usually in large quantities.

Operating a retail business generally requires rented or purchased display space and therefore requires incurring the fixed costs of running that space right from the beginning. For example, if you wanted to run a variety store, you would have to rent (or buy) a storefront location where customers can drop in during your open hours. On top of that, you will have to invest in the store's inventory, which is usually the largest cost to a retailer. The inventory can cost upward of $100,000 depending on the size and scope of the store. For these reasons, retail businesses are usually quite capital intensive and need financing from the beginning.

Wholesalers, on the other hand, generally don't have to deal with the headaches of display spaces, but they do have to maintain an inventory in a warehouse. Therefore, a wholesale business needs to incur the fixed costs associated with operating a warehouse as well as the cost of purchasing the inventory, which tends to be in larger quantities than a retailer. This also generally requires financing from the beginning.

Service business

A service business encompasses any type of business where the item purchased is not a tangible good but instead is "something that is done." Some examples of service businesses are law and accounting firms, lawn-care businesses, auto shops, and spas.

Service businesses in general require less equipment than manufacturers do, and practically no inventory. Therefore, these types of businesses are generally easier to start on a small scale and require less start-up capital. In fact, service businesses account for the majority of all small businesses in North America.

Service businesses tend to be smaller and more local than manufacturers or wholesalers, because services are provided by people and are generally not able to be shipped by parcel post. It can be logistically difficult to provide services over a wide geographic area. However, business services such as website design, accounting, and data processing are becoming the exception to this rule with the ever-expanding use of e-mail and the internet.

Eight Questions to Ask Yourself

Before you make a final decision as to what type of business to open, make sure that your personal goals and business goals are synchronized by asking yourself the following questions.

1. What are my personal financial goals?

If you want to retire a millionaire in ten years time and you are going to open a small shoe-repair shop, you may not be able to meet your goals. Analyze where you want to be in five or ten years. Do you want a larger house? Be able to travel the world? Have your retirement fully funded? You'll save yourself much grief down the road if you make sure that the type of business you start will provide you with the money you need for your intended lifestyle.

2. Will this business allow me to have the freedom I want to pursue other things?

If you start a business that is based around you being there all the time, you may not be able to pursue some of your personal goals or even to spend the time to plan and strategize for your business. Having a business that can be systematized to run without your constant presence will allow you more freedom. For a fuller discussion of systematizing your business, please see the third book in the *Numbers 101 for Small Business* series, *Managing Business Growth.*

3. Is the product or service easily marketable?

Starting a business that has a product or service that is understandable and needed by a large segment of the population is by far easier than developing a new product or service and having to both familiarize potential customers with it and, at the same time, convince them that they need it.

CASE STUDY

Craig Sesco knew from the time he was six years old that he wanted to run his own business some day. His father had owned and operated an Italian bakery since before Craig was born and Craig learned to be an entrepreneur through many years of working in the bakery, doing everything from kneading dough to running the ovens to ordering from suppliers, and, eventually, bookkeeping and cash flow forecasting.

Now Craig was 27 and he felt it was time to strike out on his own. He knew that his father had started his business by doing something he loved and that he was lucky that his passion coincided with consumer tastes, but Craig wanted to pursue a different model. He wanted to determine his best chance for commercial success and build a successful business around that.

The first process that Craig went through was to determine his personal goals. He had married his long-time love, Marnie, two years ago and they had just bought a small house for themselves and their new baby. Craig knew that he didn't want to work the crazy hours his father still put in everyday: up at 4:30 a.m. to start the stone ovens and never falling into bed before 11:00 p.m., after reconciling the day's receipts, preparing the bank deposit, and planning for the next day's purchases. Craig wanted to balance his work time with family time but still wanted to build and run a financially successful business that he could sell by the time he was 50.

Through his analysis, Craig also determined that he didn't want to run a business with huge start-up costs and large inventory levels to manage. He wanted to start small and gear up slowly as he built up more internally generated revenues.

Craig started to list the types of businesses he thought he might be successful at.

4. What are the barriers to entry for this industry?

Some industries are more difficult than others to "break into." For an extreme example, it would be incredibly difficult to start up a new auto manufacturing company to compete with Ford or Daimler Chrysler. Likewise, it would be almost impossible to set up a new company to provide telephone service to the Eastern seaboard. In both of these examples, the start-up costs are monumental (design, manufacturing equipment, and showrooms in the first instance and switching stations and telephone cabling in the second). Also, these industries are dominated by a few very large players who have built name recognition and goodwill over many years.

Ensure that you choose an industry where there is room for new participants to grow.

5. Can the business weather downturns?

Every industry has up and down times. For example, travel agents book more vacations for their customers when the economy is on an upswing than when it's in recession. A business can also be affected by how many new businesses in that industry are opening up. A flood of new providers can siphon off some of your customers, at least in the short term.

Look at whether the business you are contemplating will be able to survive external changes to its operating environment. Is your product or service easily adaptable? For example, in poor economic times, a spa will focus on advertising the basic services, such as haircuts. When times are good, it will promote higher-end services, such as massage, facials, and pedicures.

6. How easily can I expand this business?

If your goal is to grow your business over several years, it's critical to determine upfront whether the business has the potential to do that. For example, if you start a grocery store in a small town, your customer base is limited to the residents of the town. You may find it difficult to grow such a business without offering new products.

Ensure that the business has the potential to grow quickly and expand either the customer base or the range of products or services.

7. Will my product or service endure?

The only constant in business is the knowledge that consumer tastes are ever changing. The product that may have been all the rage last month may be passé this month. Think back to pet rocks, fruit-flavored potato chips, and Rubik's Cube. These items sold extremely well for an extremely short period of time. If you had built your business around one of these fads, however, you would soon have found revenues dropping precipitously and you would have been out of business quickly (unless, of course, your business hopped from fad to fad).

It's important to make sure that your service or product is not a fad and will be needed long into the future.

8.   Will I actually be able to make money with this business?

If you feel that you have found an under-serviced market niche, you need to examine why there are no other businesses serving that market. Many small businesses are able to create a toehold in an industry because large corporations would not be able to make enough profit serving that market to satisfy their investors. A small business has the advantage of lower overhead and more flexibility to move in and out of markets and can often create greater profits than its larger counterparts. However, if you want to do more than simply eke out a living running your business, make sure that the profit potential is there right from the beginning.

Chapter Summary

➡ In order to start and run a small business by yourself, you need to have skills in business building, business management, and doing what the business does.

➡ There are three main types of businesses: manufacturing, retail/wholesale, and service. When deciding what type of business to start, it's important to look at the pros and cons of running each type of business.

➡ Ensure that your personal goals fit with your plans for your business with respect to finances, freedom, and risk.

➡ It is critical to examine your choice of potential business to make sure that the product or service is viable and will stand the test of time.

Is It a Business or a Hobby?

How do you know whether your interests will produce monetary returns? We look at decision planning for your great idea.

Introduction

It's inevitable. If you're a true entrepreneur, you will eventually begin to analyze every possible venture to see if it would make a viable business. You will look at your spouse's scrapbooking project and think about the possibility of opening a scrapbooking store. You will think about ways to leverage your son's after-school lawn-cutting venture to provide service to twice the customers at half the price. When a kind-hearted jogger in the park comments on how she wishes she had a dog, you will mentally calculate how many times you would have to rent out Fido to "dogless" people to break even.

Entrepreneurs are always thinking about business. It's what sets them apart from other people and makes them visionary. There is, however, the dark side of the moon where ventures that are pure hobby are turned into businesses that are doomed to fail.

The first idea Craig came up with for his new business was operating a taxi service. He had driven a taxi part time when he was in college and he knew a lot about the business. He had even helped the taxi service's owner develop new routing procedures to lessen the drivers' down time. After drawing up some preliminary plans, however, Craig realized that owning a taxi service would violate two of his personal goals: having a balanced work/family life and not having a huge upfront investment. A taxi service would require a strong hands-on manager and he would have to fill that role until he could find someone to replace him. It also would require the purchase or lease of a central dispatch office as well as several cars. His estimates showed that he would be working approximately 60 hours per week on average and would have to find an initial investment of $120,000. He decided to leave the taxi business to someone else.

The next business opportunity Craig investigated was cheese-making. Craig had a passion for cheese-making that dated back to his days at his father's bakery. His father's brother, his Uncle Nino, had been the cheese-maker in the family. He ran a small cheese shop next door to the bakery for almost as long as Craig's father had run the bakery. Craig had worked at the bakery out of duty to his father, but he loved the occasional opportunity he got to work with his Uncle Nino making cheese. They made hard cheeses like Parmesan and Romano, and soft ones like Brie and Gouda. Craig still made cheese for his wife in a small basement room.

It made sense to Craig that he start a business based on a skill he was

It's critical to be able to tell the difference between a business and a hobby. Just because you love to go fly-fishing doesn't mean that you can make money at it.

Many highly successful entrepreneurs build and invest in businesses without having any personal interest in what the business does. They are only concerned about what growth potential the business has and its profitability. Think about Warren Buffett and Donald Trump. But there are other small-business owners who have parlayed a personal interest or hobby into a highly successful business. These business owners have, however, conducted the same analysis of the business potential as have the Buffetts and Trumps of the world. They have realized that something they enjoy doing has the potential to be a thriving business enterprise. That is not so, however, with all hobbies.

What Is the Difference Between a Business and a Hobby?

Let's look at the characteristics of a business versus a hobby.

Characteristics of a business:

- Designed on sound business principles
- Tailored to the needs of its customers
- Enjoyment garnered from building or managing the business
- Reasonable expectation of increasing profit over time

Characteristics of a hobby:

- Tailored to the needs of the hobbyist
- Incurs high costs compared to potential return
- Designed based on desires of the hobbyist
- Enjoyment garnered from performing the service
- Little or no expectation of increasing profits over time

A sound business is always centered on its customers. The reason for its existence is to serve its customer base, and customer satisfaction is the measure of its success. An entrepreneur who builds and manages a small business derives his or her pleasure from the *process* of providing the product or service as opposed to the actual provision.

Let's use a deep sea diving outfit to demonstrate the difference between a business and a hobby. Maria owns a boat and several sets of dive gear. She has been doing deep sea diving almost all of her life and she wants to take others out to teach them how to do it. If this is simply a hobby for Maria, she will take people out to dive sites that she particularly enjoys and will purchase dive equipment and other supplies without regard to analyzing the cost versus the benefit of such expenditures. She will set hours that are convenient to her and will only book tours during that time. The enjoyment that she gets is in the actual diving itself. She wants to share her hobby with others and has no interest in hiring others to perform the work or in growing or selling the business.

On the other hand, if this is a true business, Maria will spend time upfront "crunching the numbers": calculating her break-even point by figuring out how many tours she needs to book to cover the capital cost of the boat and its related maintenance, as well as the dive equipment. She will research what tourists are most interested in when they book a diving tour and will adjust her availability to the most popular tourist seasons. If the growth potential is present to allow it, she will most likely hire another experienced diver in order to be able to run more tours. The enjoyment that Maria will get from building this business is in seeing it grow and serve its customers. She will know that she is building something that will outlast her and that she can sell when she wants to pursue other ventures.

It's definitely true that many successful entrepreneurs have translated their personal interests into highly successful businesses, and potentially, you can too. However, it's always important to make sure that your reasons for starting the business extend beyond the pure enjoyment of doing what the business does.

It's Not Always about the Money

Now that we've discussed why you should be extremely careful in trying to make your hobby your business, it's important to make the point that you can still have a hobby. Not everything you do has to produce profit. In fact, the most fun part about a hobby is that you do not have to worry about things like profitability or the satisfaction of others. Trying to turn your hobby into a business may not only be unprofitable, but may also make you end up hating the hobby. Entrepreneurs and small-business owners need to have more interests than just their businesses in order to maintain a balanced lifestyle. If you do nothing except keep your nose to the grindstone in your business all day, everyday, think about what an uninteresting person you'd be!

CASE STUDY
continued

good at and loved. He quickly came to realize, however, that he was following the same path as his father, without the assurance of success. High-quality cheeses appealed only to a small segment of the market, and Craig would once again have be at the business all the time as he was the one with the skill to produce the cheese. Rather reluctantly, Craig shelved the idea of building a cheese-making empire.

Chapter Summary

➡ Entrepreneurs are continually assessing potential ventures to see if they would make profitable businesses, but they run the risk of trying to turn a purely pleasurable pastime into an unprofitable business.

➡ Although many successful small-business owners have parlayed their personal interests into successful businesses, many more build and grow a business without a personal interest in the underlying activities of the business.

➡ Businesses are always run for the benefit of the customers, whereas hobbies are undertaken for the benefit of the hobbyist.

➡ Small-business owners should still pursue hobbies and personal interests to maintain a balance between their personal and business lives.

Build or Buy?

Is it better to build a business from the ground up or to purchase an existing business? This chapter outlines the considerations.

Introduction

If you want to become a small-business owner, there are two ways to do it: you can either build a business from the ground up or you can buy an existing business. Each strategy has its pros and cons. The strategy that's right for you will depend partly on your motivation for being a small-business owner and partly on cash flow considerations.

If your motivation for starting a small business is that you derive pleasure from building something from nothing, you are more likely to garner that pleasure from building your own business, although you may also take pleasure in buying a business and molding it into your image. On the other hand, your interests may lie more on the managing side and you would therefore prefer to walk into an existing business and begin to run it.

CASE STUDY

It was then that the perfect business quite literally fell into Craig's lap. It was his second wedding anniversary and he had taken his wife out for dinner at an upscale French bistro. As they were enjoying their desserts, the power went out, an occurrence that was becoming all too common on the Eastern seaboard where they lived.

There were auxiliary lights in the bistro, just enough for Craig to see most of the patrons leaving, despite the servers' quick efforts to light candles on every table. The server looking after Craig and Marnie's table told them that some were leaving because they were uncomfortable with the blackout and some because the bistro couldn't accept credit cards because its system worked solely on electricity. Craig sipped his wine and contemplated the money that the restaurant was losing because of the blackout, when, quite unexpectedly, the busboy tripped in the aisle and dumped a half-eaten plate of gnocchi in Craig's lap.

"I'm so sorry," the busboy said, cleaning up the mess. "I couldn't see where I was going. I hate these blackouts."

Craig wondered aloud to Marnie how many businesses were facing the same problem at that moment along the Seaboard. Business was being lost because of the lights not being on. Craig then recalled an article he had recently read in the paper about a new company called Green Power Inc. that was selling solar and wind energy solutions to both businesses and residences. Craig hadn't given much thought to the concept until now, but suddenly realized the benefits to both business owners and homeowners.

Cash flow also plays a part in your decision. If you are purchasing goodwill along with the net assets of the business, you will be paying more than if you simply purchase assets and start from scratch. Buying an existing business is usually the more expensive option. However, a business that is already up and running may provide you with profits and a management income earlier. This may offset the initial cost. When you build a small business from scratch, it may take months or even a year before you hit the break-even point, much less make profit that you can put in your pocket. In the meantime, you will be investing a large amount of your time building the enterprise without remuneration, and this is a cost that you must figure into your calculations as well.

Let's look at the pros and cons of building a business from scratch versus those of buying an existing business.

Building a Business from Scratch

When you build a business from scratch, you will start with nothing but the tiniest grain of an idea. You will spend months or longer mapping out that idea, running cash flow scenarios, doing market and competitive analysis, writing a business plan and a management operating plan, and working on the business's vision and mission statements. You will be meeting with bankers, accountants, lawyers, and financial planners as you build your external advisory team.

You will most likely open your doors before you take in the first dollar in revenues, and you will take the enormous leap of faith that customers will actually want what you are selling the way you had it laid out in the plan.

It sounds scary but designing and building the business that exists in your head can be an extremely fulfilling and gratifying experience. So much so, that many successful entrepreneurs design and build businesses, then sell them once they're up and running. Then they start all over again and build another one.

Here are some of the pros of building a business from scratch:

- You can design internal systems the way you want them to work right from the beginning.
- It can be less expensive than buying an existing operation.
- There is no risk of acquiring the previous owners' liabilities or having to satisfy pre-existing warranties.

- You can manage staffing needs more carefully (i.e., you don't inherit employees that are sub-par and/or difficult to fire).

There are some cons to building a business from scratch:

- It can be more difficult and expensive to attract investors. Because the venture doesn't exist yet, it will be riskier for them.
- It can take longer to generate profits than with an existing business.
- It can take a long time to build name recognition and goodwill with customers.
- There is a much greater risk of failure than with a business that has a proven track record.

Buying an Existing Business

Buying an existing business is, in general, less of a risk for you as the major investor. You have the opportunity to watch the business in action and you will be able to access the historical financial information to determine patterns such as growth rate, profitability, and solvency. You know that you will be able to generate a return on your investment almost immediately as well as be remunerated for your management role in the business (and perhaps also your operational role).

You may also choose to buy a business if you want to quickly introduce a new product to an existing customer base before there are too many competitors in the market. For example, if you have developed a brand new print-on-demand self-serve book station, you may want to have instant access to a thriving bookstore's customers before copycats come on the market.

Here are some of the pros of buying an existing business:

- It can be easier to obtain external financing than if you build a business from scratch because the business has a track record.
- You can market your existing products to a new customer base.
- It is easier to manage an existing business model and fine-tune it than build it from the ground up.
- You can generate profits right from the purchase date.

CASE STUDY
continued

The next morning (several hours after the lights came back on), Craig called Green Power Inc. to find out more information. Craig met with the owner that afternoon and, two weeks later, Craig was presented with an offer to buy into a new offshoot of Green Power Inc. aimed at the residential market. Craig would have a 50 percent ownership stake in the new business with Gordon, the current owner of Green Power. Craig's responsibilities would be those of the general manager; he would run the day-to-day operations and would head up all strategic and operational planning. For this, he would be paid a salary of $67,000 plus would receive dividends as an owner of the company.

Craig spent the following week with his accountant, analyzing the offer and the potential return. He compared it to the cost of starting up his own alternative energy company and determined that the cost of starting from scratch would outweigh the additional profit from owning the entire business. He would not only have to invest in all of the marketing materials, but he would have to develop the necessary expertise in alternative energy. Craig's best opportunity would be to buy into the new offshoot of the existing company.

- You can continue the business with the existing goodwill and name recognition.

There are some cons to buying an existing business:

- You may be inheriting the hidden headaches of the previous owner.

- You may be inheriting "negative goodwill" if the business had a bad name in the community.

- It may take as long to reshape the business the way you want it as it would to have started a new business from scratch.

- The customers you are "buying" may have only been loyal to the former owner and may choose not to stay on as customers when you take over.

Financial Considerations in the Build-versus-Buy Decision

Once you have taken into consideration your personal goals and your tolerance of risk, the decision to buy versus build a business comes down to a financial one. There are many ways to analyze a purchase decision, but we will look at the most common: the discounted cash flow method.

Discounted cash flow analysis (DCF) helps us to look at a purchase decision and figure out at what point our cash inflows (revenue) match and then exceed our cash outflows (operating and financing costs). DCF takes into consideration the important fact that the timing of the inflows and outflows of cash are different. A dollar received three years from now is worth less than a dollar that we have to spend today. This is called the time value of money and is the basis of DCF analysis. For more information on cash flows, please refer to *Financial Management 101,* the second book in the *Numbers 101 for Small Business* series.

Let's look at an example to see DCF in action:

You have been offered the opportunity to purchase a sign-making company for $225,000. You have already talked to your bank manager and she is willing to finance $175,000 but you will have to use $50,000 of your own savings to finance the rest. You have been thinking about starting up a similar type of company for some time and you want to compare the cash flows of purchasing an existing business versus building one from scratch.

Considering a start-up business

You have put together a cash flow projection for the proposed start-up company. The five-year cash flow projection is shown in Sample 1.

In this start-up company, you would be investing $50,000 of your own money in order to finance the start-up costs of $18,860 and the cash shortfalls in years one and two ($17,060 and $7,250 respectively). By year three, the company is projected to have a cash surplus, which grows annually up to year five.

You can see that before you even open the doors, you will have to invest $18,860 into the company. Most of that money goes towards buying the sign-making equipment and inventory. Further investments in equipment will have to be made every year as the company starts increasing sales.

How can we evaluate whether or not this option would be a sound investment? There are many methods of decision analysis. The method we'll consider here is to look at discounted cash flows. This method allows us to come up with an annualized return on investment. Remember that you will invest $50,000 into this venture. You could have taken that $50,000 and put it in the stock market or invested it in bonds. Both of those activities would have generated a return. In the same manner, we can look at the return from this start-up business.

The annualized return on investment is simply the amount of funds left over to put in the owners' pocket after all of the business expenses are paid. Note that we are talking about *all* the expenses, which includes remuneration for all work done in the business. In this scenario, you will be paid a management salary of $48,000 in years one and two, $59,000 in years three and four, and $63,000 in year five.

If, however, your cash flow projections don't allow for you to be paid for your labor, calculating a return on investment is rather meaningless. It means that, not only are you investing money, you are investing your labor for free (this is known as "sweat equity"). In this scenario, however, you are being paid for your efforts and therefore can look at how much you're getting for your $50,000 investment.

SAMPLE 1
CASH FLOW PROJECTION FOR A START-UP BUSINESS

	On start up	Year 1	Year 2	Year 3	Year 4	Year 5
Cash receipts		163,000	197,000	259,000	375,000	425,000
Inventory purchases	4,965	70,090	84,710	111,370	161,250	182,750
Advertising		7,950	7,275	6,950	6,750	6,750
Bank charges		1,250	1,250	1,250	1,250	1,250
Office expenses		5,310	6,150	7,630	10,995	11,865
Professional fees	1,275	2,200	2,400	2,600	2,950	3,250
Rent	2,000	24,000	25,350	27,695	48,000	50,050
Supplies	975	6,000	6,500	7,100	7,640	7,950
Telephone & utilities	395	3,600	3,75	4,150	6,525	6,750
Vehicle expenses		2,400	2,640	2,980	4,525	4,745
Management salary		48,000	48,000	59,000	59,000	63,000
Wages & benefits		6,515	13,225	15,000	32,000	36,500
Purchase of capital equipment	9,250	2,745	3,000	3,625	8,525	3,750
Total inflows	-	163,000	197,000	259,000	375,000	425,000
Total outflows	18,860	180,060	204,250	249,350	349,410	378,610
Net cash inflows (outflows)	(18,860)	(17,060)	(7,250)	9,650	25,590	46,390
Total invested by owner		50,000				
Annualized ROI		5.27%				

The net cash available for distribution to the owners looks like this:

On start up	($18,860)	
Year 1	(17,060)	
Year 2	(7,250)	
Year 3	9,650	(YEA!! Positive cash flow!)
Year 4	25,590	
Year 5	46,390	

We also know from the above discussion that a dollar received or spent tomorrow is worth less than a dollar received or spent today. This means that we will want to discount this stream of cash flows back to today, to the present value of the dollar, to make sure we are comparing apples to apples, so to speak. The first thing that we need to do is to find a meaningful interest rate at which to discount the cash flows. After speaking with your banker, you know that you can borrow from the bank at 10 percent, so we will use this rate to do our discounting. There is a formula to calculate the present value of a dollar, but we will take the easy way and use a table. This table is found in Appendix 1. Match the interest rate (in this case, 10 percent) at the top with the periods along the side, and read off the corresponding factor for each period. To calculate how much your future cash flows are worth today, multiply each cash flow by the factor for that period.

Let's follow through the example, using a portion of the present value table reproduced below:

Period	10%
1	0.9091
2	0.8264
3	0.7513
4	0.6830
5	0.6209

This table tells us, for example, that if we are going to receive a dollar a year from now, it is only really worth 90.91¢ today. You can see that, as we go farther into the future, the worth of that same dollar becomes less and less. We have to bring all of our cash flows back to a common point: today. Sample 2 has completed the calculations.

This tells us that, over five years, the company will generate $13,171 in net positive discounted cash flow. We also know that

SAMPLE 2
DISCOUNTED CASH FLOWS FOR A START-UP BUSINESS

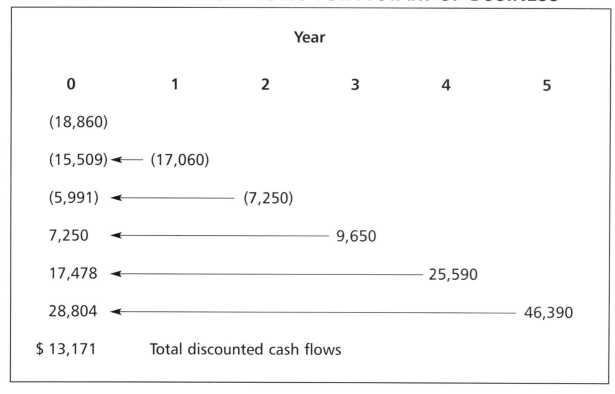

Year

0	1	2	3	4	5
(18,860)					
(15,509) ← (17,060)					
(5,991) ← (7,250)					
7,250 ← 9,650					
17,478 ← 25,590					
28,804 ← 46,390					

$ 13,171   Total discounted cash flows

you will have to invest $50,000 to get that cash flow. The calculation for your average annualized return on investment (ROI) is:

ROI = net cash flow/investment/# years

Therefore, your ROI in this scenario will be:

ROI = 13,171/50,000/5 = 5.27%

Your average annual return on your initial investment is 5.27 percent. This calculation is helpful in deciding whether to invest the money in this business or another business or another type of investment altogether. It is important to realize, however, that after year five, the cash flow is in permanently better position as the company matures. Therefore, by the time year six rolls around, the business will be generating in excess of $46,000 in net profit; a much higher return for the initial investment. Return on investment analysis will change depending on the time frame used.

Considering a business purchase

Let's look at the cash flows for the projected business purchase and see how they compare to the start-up business using the same analysis.

The purchase price for the business is $225,000. The bank is willing to lend $175,000 at 10 percent and you will have to invest $50,000 of your own money. This company has been in business for many years and therefore has mature cash flows already, similar to those in your projections for year five of the start-up company. The cash flow projections are shown in Sample 3.

There are a few important items to note here:

- The purchase of capital equipment is more regular than in the build scenario and of similar amounts from year to year. The company already owns its equipment (that's part of what you're buying) but some will need to be replaced every year as it wears out or becomes obsolete.

- The revenues are growing by a lesser percentage than with the start-up company. This company already has a mature market and grows at a slower pace than a business in its infancy (for a more in-depth discussion of the life cycle of a business, please refer to the third book in the *Numbers 101 for Small Business* series, *Managing Business Growth*).

- The net cash flow of the business operations is much higher than that of the start-up, but we have to figure in the payments of principal and interest on the bank loan before we can calculate the return on the owner's investment.

- In both scenarios (start-up and purchase), the management salary is the same and therefore does not become a factor in the decision-making process. However, if the salaries in each were different, you would have to "normalize" them. This means that you would have to recast the numbers of one or the other (or both!) projections to reflect the amount of management salary that you intend to take from the business, otherwise you are not comparing apples to apples.

Take a look at the discounted cash flows for the purchased business in Sample 4.

This tells us that the total discounted cash flows of $24,192 are higher than in the start-up scenario ($13,171). However, if the amount of the original investment had been more in the purchase scenario, this still may not be the better option. The only way to

SAMPLE 3
CASH FLOW PROJECTION FOR A BUSINESS PURCHASE

Purchase price = $225,000

	Year 1	Year 2	Year 3	Year 4	Year 5
Cash receipts	412,500	420,000	447,000	464,000	471,500
Inventory purchases	177,375	180,600	192,210	201,670	204,250
Advertising	4,150	4,200	4,200	4,350	4,400
Bank charges	1,950	1,950	2,050	2,195	2,235
Office expenses	12,540	13,250	13,985	15,010	15,775
Professional fees	3,250	3,500	3,750	4,000	4,250
Rent	52,000	53,750	56,450	59,000	62,450
Supplies	8,250	8,250	8,495	8,540	8,725
Telephone & utilities	6,250	6,550	6,745	6,985	7,140
Vehicle expenses	4,950	5,150	5,300	5,350	5,615
Management salary	48,000	48,000	59,000	59,000	63,000
Wages & benefits	37,500	38,500	40,250	41,950	43,745
Purchase of capital equipment	3,750	3,750	3,895	3,895	3,975
Interest on line of credit	-	-	-	-	-
Total inflows	412,500	420,000	447,000	464,000	471,500
Total outflows	359,965	367,450	396,330	411,945	425,560
Net cash inflows/(outflows)	52,535	52,550	50,670	52,055	45,940
Interest & principal payments	44,620	44,620	44,620	44,620	44,620
Net return to owner	7,915	7,930	6,050	7,435	1,320
Total invested by owner	50,000				
Annualized ROI	9.68%				

SAMPLE 4
DISCOUNTED CASH FLOWS FOR A BUSINESS PURCHASE

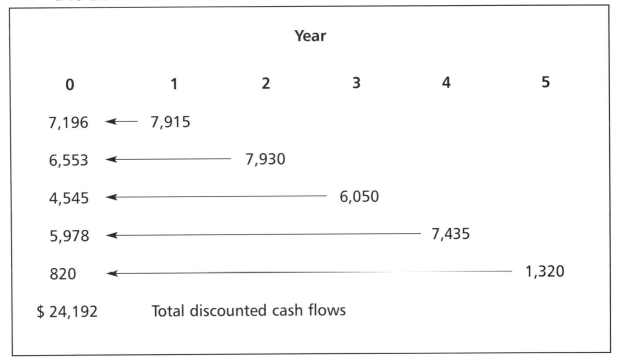

accurately compare between the two is to complete the ROI calculation. In the purchase scenario, the calculation works out to:

ROI = net cash flow/investment/# years

ROI = 24,192/50,000/5 = 9.68%

The option to purchase the existing business yields a return on your $50,000 investment of 9.68 percent, while the start-up would only yield 5.27 percent. All other things being equal, purchasing the existing business makes more financial sense.

Just to reinforce the concepts, try calculating the ROI analysis if all cash flows were the same but you had to invest $95,000 to purchase the existing business. Would this be the better option? The answer is no. If you have to invest $95,000 of your own money to purchase this business, the ROI drops from 9.68 percent to 5 percent, thereby giving you less reward for a higher risk than starting a business from scratch.

What's Right for You?

As we have discussed in this chapter, there are many considerations when you are deciding whether to start a business from scratch or to purchase an existing business. Many of those considerations relate back to your personal and business goals and will be determined by the reasons that you want to be a business owner in the first place. You will need to balance those goals with solid financial analysis to determine which option will give you the best opportunity for success.

Chapter Summary

➡ Building a business, managing a business, and working in a business are three very different activities and it is important that you analyze which ones are most important to you before you start any business.

➡ The two ways to become a business owner are to build a business from scratch or to buy an existing business. Each has its own pros and cons.

➡ Calculating the discounted cash flows of each business option will ensure that you are properly comparing future cash flows with each other.

➡ The return on investment is the amount of funds available to the owners of a business after all the expenses have been paid.

Getting Your Personal Finances in Order

Before you start your business, you need to make sure that the rest of your financial house is in order.

Introduction

One of your personal goals may be to make enough money out of your business to be wealthy, or at least be comfortable. You may see starting a small business as a way out of your current financial woes. This is a very dangerous way of thinking. You are likely to manage your business the same way you manage your personal life. If you have problems managing personal debt, that may be true in your business as well. If you don't know how much insurance you need to cover off your personal assets, you may under-insure your business assets and be exposed to unknowing risk.

It is important to clean up your own financial house before you start or buy a business. A bank will undoubtedly review your personal financial situation before lending the business any money. Suppliers who extend your business credit may also want to review your credit history and personal wealth. Your personal financial situation might end up crippling your business's ability to attract

CASE STUDY

Craig and Marnie discussed the implications of being business owners. Craig was looking forward to the adventure but Marnie had some reservations.

"We still have so much credit card debt. I doubt the bank will lend us the money we need to buy into this business."

"Why don't we go talk to the bank about consolidating our credit cards?" said Craig. "We have some equity in the house that we're not using so maybe the bank can help us out."

The next day, Craig met with his accountant, Vivian. Vivian confirmed Marnie's suspicions that they needed to re-arrange some of their personal finances before they could approach a bank or another lender for funding to purchase the business.

Vivian recommended that they increase their mortgage to be able to pay off their revolving debt, namely, their credit cards.

"Lowering your revolving debt will increase your credit score," Vivian said, "and that will make a bank more likely to lend you some of the capital you will need to invest in this business."

Craig was more confident than ever that he was going to be able to buy into this business, but Vivian brought up some other issues that he hadn't thought about.

"What will happen if you can't work in the business? How will you support Marnie and the baby?" Vivian asked.

Craig hadn't thought about this before. He scheduled an appointment for the next day with his insurance agent to ensure that he would have adequate coverage for any adversity that may arise.

investment capital. From a more practical perspective, if you don't have your personal financial life under control now, where will you find the time to do so while building your business empire?

Integrating your personal financial planning into your business planning gives you a more holistic and global view of your entire financial life and will help you to define your financial and retirement goals.

Your Retirement Goals

So you've decided to jump into the role of entrepreneur. You have fantastic vision and insight and are looking forward to managing and growing your business for a long time to come. Have you thought about what happens then? Do you still plan on coming into the office every day at 9 a.m. when you're 60? 70? How about 90? Most likely, you have at least a vague concept of what you want to do when you're older. You may even have decided that you want to make enough money in your business to retire when you're 40 or 50.

Analyzing your retirement goals involves more than just vague concepts. It is the basis for your business and personal financial plans. If you're planning that your business will provide you a steady income for your working life and then a small gain on sale when you sell, you need to ensure that these funds will be sufficient to meet your financial needs when you retire, otherwise, you'll need to keep working longer than you had anticipated.

The minimum financial goal for your retirement is to be financially independent. Financial independence means that you will be able to live off your financial capital for the rest of your life without working, if you wish.

Let's look at an example to illustrate how this works. We will walk through a simple example, which will exclude some complexities that exist in real life, like the impact of taxes and income from other sources such as pensions. When you are making your retirement calculations, I highly recommend that you do so with the assistance of your accountant or independent financial adviser (by independent, I mean someone who doesn't make commissions from the products he or she sells you).

Start by getting a handle on how much income you need per year to live on after you have retired. Keep in mind that you will have (hopefully!) no debt or mortgage payment and that your assets will be owned free and clear. You will simply have your ongoing living expenses (e.g., property taxes, utilities, food, clothing, medical) and any money that you need to carry out your retirement dreams, such as travel costs. Your post-retirement income needs are likely to be much lower than your current ones. Let's say that you have decided that you want to have $50,000 per year to live on when you retire. You are 35 right now and plan on retiring when you are 60. Therefore you have 25 years to save for your retirement. You want to make sure that you are being conservative and plan to live until you are 90 years old, so you will need the $50,000 per year for 30 years. You have life insurance and therefore have no need to have any cash left at death. There are two questions that need to be answered mathematically:

- How much will you need to have saved by the time you are 60 in order to meet your income requirements? and

- How much will you have to put into your retirement fund each year between now and age 60 to have that amount available?

We will use a 6 percent average return for our calculations.

How much will you need at age 60?

This is simply a mathematical calculation that involves the present value of an annuity. The full table used for the calculation is in Appendix 2. To calculate, you multiply the annual income required ($50,000) by the appropriate factor in the table. Multiplying by this factor takes into account the fact that future dollars are not worth as much as today's dollars. At an interest rate of 6 percent and 30 annual periods, the factor is 13.765. Therefore, the amount that you need to have in retirement savings by the time you are 60 is $50,000 X 13.765 = $688,250. In most cases, this won't have to come solely from savings. You may have pension income from a job or a 401K. Your business will also likely have a value when you sell it to retire. Be careful about making these assumptions too rosy in case they don't happen. In this scenario, we will assume that the entire retirement fund is coming from savings.

How much do you have to put away between now and retirement?

You know that you will need $688,250 by the time you turn 60. You have 25 years to save that amount (at an assumed 6 percent rate of return). How much will you have to sock away every year to meet your goal? Again, the formula is simple mathematics. We now use the future value of an annuity to calculate the payments. The full table is reproduced in Appendix 3. Using a 6 percent interest rate and 25 periods, the factor is 54.865. You divide the required retirement fund amount by the factor to come up with the annual payments into the fund. In this case, it is $688,250/54.865 = $12,544 per year that you will have to tuck into your retirement fund in order to meet your retirement goals.

So, why is this information important to you now, when you are starting up your business? It's important when you set your business financial goals. You now know that if you want to meet your personal retirement goals, you will have to draw enough from your business not only to cover your current living expenses, but also an extra $12,544 per year to fund your retirement. Many small-business owners have retirement goals that are at odds with what they are making from their businesses. The earlier you integrate these goals, the more likely you will achieve them.

Use the template in Worksheet 1 to begin to contemplate your own retirement goals.

The Concept of Net Wealth

How much are you really worth? You may be drawing a large salary from your business but if it all gets spent on current expenses, it doesn't add to the value of your possessions. One of the most important measures in your personal financial planning is your net wealth. This is simply your assets minus your liabilities. Over time, your assets should grow and your liabilities should decrease, which decreases the risks you are exposed to and increases your financial stability. Ultimately, your net wealth is what you have to live on and then to pass on to the next generation.

It doesn't have to be onerous to track your net wealth. You can simply write down your best estimate of the value of all of your assets and then the payout amount of all of your liabilities (i.e., the amount of money it would take to settle up your debts). You may also choose to use a software program that will track not only your net wealth but also your income and spending. It may also track your retirement savings. Popular programs such as Intuit's *Quicken* or *Microsoft Money* make the tracking easy. If you do this on a regular basis (monthly or at least annually) you will be able to see how your wealth increases over time.

Your assets may include:

- Cash
- Portfolio investments (bonds, stocks, etc.)
- Your home

WORKSHEET 1
RETIREMENT PLANNING

A. Current age: _____

B. Planned retirement age: _____

C. Years to retirement (B minus A): _____

D. Expected life span in years: _____

E. No. of years retirement income required (D minus B): _____

F. Amount of annual income required at retirement: _____

G. Estimated annual return on investment: _____

H. Factor from table in Appendix 3 using rate in (G) and no. years in (E):_____

I. Income in (F) multiplied by factor in (H): _____ Amount needed

J. Factor from table in Appendix 4 using rate in (G) and no. years in (C): _____

K. Amount from (I) divided by factor in (J): _____ Amount to fund per year

- Other real estate (cottages, vacant land, rental properties, etc.)
- Vehicles
- Savings (including retirement accounts and college funds)
- Your business

Your liabilities may include:

- Mortgage
- Credit card balances
- Personal loans
- Car loan

The higher your net wealth, the more likely a bank will look favorably upon your business as it needs financing.

Debt Management

In order to make sure that you will manage your business debt appropriately, it's important to first get a handle on your personal debt.

There is an old adage about good debt versus bad debt. Bad debt is defined as any debt you undertake to purchase things that do not grow in value. This would apply if you're using your credit card or line of credit to go on a vacation or buy living room furniture or a car. Good debt, on the other hand, is debt that's incurred to invest in things that will grow in value, such as your home, other real estate, and stock market investments. Conventional wisdom says that bad debt should be avoided or paid down as quickly as possible, but good debt is acceptable and should even be pursued.

The problem with this outlook is that it does not recognize that debt means risk for you, regardless of what that debt buys you. Any time you have required payments to make, you run the risk of not being able to pay them and thereby becoming insolvent or even bankrupt. When you borrow to invest, either in real estate or in bonds or the stock market, there is no guarantee that these investments will increase in the short term, which is when you have to make the payments. There is a danger that, if the value of the investment drops below what is owed on the loan, the loan will be called. In that situation, even if the investment is sold, you will still owe money.

Another investment "nugget" suggests that paying interest on investment loans in order to build investment assets is a good idea.

As we have discussed above, all investment entails risk, whereas paying down your debts can give you a greater return on an after-tax basis. Let's look at an example:

Your spouse has received a $5,000 bonus from his employer. You are considering whether to invest that in your investment account or to pay off the last of your credit card debt. Currently, the long-term investment return from stock investments is about 6 percent. You will have to pay taxes on part of that income, however, and therefore, your after-tax return may be as low as 3 or 4 percent. On the other hand, your credit card company charges 19 percent. Paying off that card will give you a 19 percent return after tax, as there are no tax implications of paying off debt. Not only is your return much higher, paying off debt gives you that return risk free. It's a guaranteed return. Always keep this in mind when trying to decide what to do with windfalls and extra money in your budget.

I'm certainly not advocating that you do not have any personal debt whatsoever. Simply keep in mind that debt equals risk. As a small-business owner, you will be exposed to plenty of risk as it is, without adding to it on the personal side. Here are some things that you can do to get a handle on your personal debt situation:

1. List out all of your personal debts, the terms left on them, and the interest rate.

2. Rank your debts by highest to lowest interest rates. You will find that the highest interest rate debts are generally credit cards, retail cards, rent-to-own situations, and payday loans. The more the debt is secured by underlying assets, the lower the rate will be. For example, because the bank can take back your home if you do not make the mortgage payments, mortgage rates tend to be lower because the risk to the bank (not to you!) is lower.

3. Review your budget and calculate how much you can set aside for debt repayment.

4. Make a formal debt repayment plan. For each debt, you should know how long it will take to pay off (not just the minimum required by the lender). Start with the highest interest rate debts and pay them off as quickly as possible.

5. Stick to your budget! Make sure that you make the payments that you have calculated every month in order to be out of debt when you have planned to be.

Your Credit History

In North America, almost every person who has ever borrowed money from an institution will have a credit report on file with one of the major credit bureaus. This report will have your borrowing and employment history, including amounts owing, how quickly you have repaid past loans, whether any payments are overdue, and whether a lender has ever had to turn any of your debt over to a collection agency in the past. Any past bankruptcies will also show up on this report. This information culminates in your credit score, which is used by lenders to predict whether or not you are a good credit risk. Having a poor score can not only ensure that you are denied future credit but you may also have to pay a much higher interest rate to offset what the lender perceives as your increased risk.

You have a right to have access to your own credit reports and it is highly recommended that you review it on a regular basis, as often as yearly. It's important for you to know how a future lender will view you. There is also the possibility that your credit report contains inaccurate information, which you should have corrected as soon as possible to avoid it impacting your credit-worthiness.

Your personal credit history will also come into play when you start your small business. Most banks and leasing companies will check your personal credit score to make sure that you pay both your personal and business debts on time. This will matter greatly when you apply for a business line of credit or for a lease arrangement for your equipment.

Make sure your personal credit history is as clean and in order as possible before you contemplate starting your business. It will save you many headaches down the road.

In the United States, there are three national credit reporting agencies for individuals and it is important to see your credit information from all three:

- Equifax: www.equifax.com
- TransUnion: www.transunion.com
- Experian: www.experian.com

In Canada, there are two national reporting agencies:

- Equifax: www.equifax.com
- TransUnion: www.tuc.ca

Insuring Your Assets

Insurance isn't a topic that many people give much thought to. But it goes hand-in-hand with our discussion about risk. In its most simple terms, insurance (for a fee) protects us against the risk of losing our assets. As a small-business owner, having adequate insurance will become vitally important. Let's have a look at the major categories of insurance that you should consider.

Life insurance

What will happen when you die? Basically, anyone who is dependent upon you bringing in income will no longer have that source of income. This will be especially important if you have a spouse and children. The family home must still be maintained and the children's education accounts must still be funded. It may be impossible for your spouse to carry the burden alone when you are gone. If this is the case, it's imperative that you have life insurance to replace your lost income, at least until the children are grown and self-sufficient. If, however, you are single and have no other dependents, life insurance is not a necessity and the premiums that you would otherwise pay might be better off in an investment account.

There are many types of life insurance, some of which have an investment component to them. A discussion of the options available is beyond the scope of this book and should be discussed with your accountant or independent financial adviser.

How much life insurance do you need? You should be able to review your current spending budget and compare it to the after-tax income of your spouse (remember that he or she will most likely keep working). The shortfall between the expenses and the income will need to be funded through life insurance. Another alternative is to insure for the amount of your debts, including your mortgage. Then, upon your death, your spouse will only have to pay ongoing living expenses and not have any debt payments.

Mortgage insurance

Mortgage insurance will pay off the outstanding balance of your mortgage when you die. However, the premiums for most policies are set based on the amount owing when the policy is set up. So, for example, you may owe $150,000 now on your mortgage and will pay premiums based on that. In ten years, when you die, you may only owe $10,000 and that would be the amount paid out on the policy. In general, the premiums for mortgage insurance tend to be high compared to the payout. Mortgage insurance can be replaced with additional life insurance for a much lower cost in many cases, and should be discussed with your accountant or independent financial planner.

Property and casualty insurance

This type of insurance protects you from the loss of your belongings, such as your house and its contents, your car, and any other physical assets you may have. Many property and casualty policies also contain a liability component, so that, for example, if someone slips on the ice and breaks a leg on your front steps, your insurance will pay.

Your insurance company will have standards as to how much insurance they will provide based on their assessed market value of your assets. You should ensure, though, that what will be paid out in insurance will at least cover any debt secured by that asset. For example, let's say you have a car on which you are making monthly payments. The insured value of the car is $6,000 but you still owe $7,500 on it. If the car is totaled, the financing company will immediately call the loan and you will have to dig up the excess $1,500 from somewhere to cover it.

When assessing whether your belongings are adequately covered by property and casualty insurance, make sure that you have considered any special collections you might own, such as stamps, art, hockey cards, or antiques. These types of assets are generally not covered under the standard policy and you may have to take out a special rider on them.

Health insurance

Health insurance is one area in which the majority of people are under-insured. It may be tempting to just assume that you will be healthy until you retire, but that is dangerous thinking. If your health fails, your ability to earn income may disappear, along with your plans for retirement.

As a small-business owner, health insurance is essential as you will not be able to rely on any employer- or government-funded health plans. There are two major coverages that you need to consider. The first is that you will not have your income any longer. As a small-business owner, you will have to hire someone to do the work that you once did or you may even have to close the doors, but either way, you will have to replace your former income. The second is that you may have ongoing medical and long-term care expenses in the future. For example, you may have to hire a private care nurse to attend to your medical needs.

There are many forms of health insurance. Some include coverage for drugs and dental expenses, some pay out a lump sum when you are diagnosed with a critical illness, and some provide ongoing payments for your lifetime. Discuss coverage with your financial adviser or insurance specialist to make sure that you will be able to continue to meet your personal and business financial goals in the event of serious illness.

Chapter Summary

➡ Before you jump into the role of business owner, it's important to first get your personal finances in shape.

➡ Reviewing your personal financial and retirement goals will help when you plan your business to ensure that all of your goals are in alignment.

➡ Getting your personal debt under control will help with your borrowing capacity in your business and will help you to manage your business debt more effectively.

➡ Having adequate insurance on all of your assets will help you to financially weather any catastrophic event.

Chapter

5

Setting Your Business Goals

W hat do you want from your business? Money? Status? Security? We look at the various goals of entrepreneurs and how to align your plan with your goals.

Introduction

We have spent considerable time so far discussing the personal side of your financial life because it forms a critical pillar to the success of your business. In this chapter, we begin to look at your business goals and how to set up your initial business plan.

By this point, you have considered what type of business you want to start and why you want to be an entrepreneur (Chapter 1). You have also thought about which opportunity will be best for you: starting a business from scratch or buying an existing business (Chapter 3).

Now, you will need to start planning your business, including what your projected cash flows will be, when you will start to turn a profit, and how you will get out of your business when you're ready to do other things.

CASE STUDY

Craig's next job was to work on the presentation to the investors. He and his partner, Gordon, had decided on the name EarthPower for their new company but had not been able to agree on much else. He quickly realized that, not only did he have to figure out how to present the company to outsiders, but he also had to figure out what the company would look like so that he could work on the strategic plan.

Craig and Gordon booked off an entire day to work on the vision for the company. Once they started to discuss the products and services that they would offer their customers, Craig realized they had entirely different visions for the company. Craig called Vivian that afternoon for her advice and she recommended that the partners engage in a mediated visioning session.

"What's that?" Craig asked, perplexed.

"A visioning session will help the two of you to come to a consensus as to what the business will look like and what products and services it will offer. Determining that upfront will help to deflect problems down the road. You both will have a good handle on what the business is and does."

"But what does 'mediated' mean?" Craig asked.

"Mediated means that a third party — in this case, me — will be a participant in the talks and will help to balance out both views. You can imagine what would happen in an unmediated discussion if one partner always puts forward his opinion without ever letting the other partner speak. It's not very effective. Once we've had the visioning session, we'll start on the business plan."

Craig rubbed his forehead. This was starting to sound like real work.

We will start by talking about money.

Chasing the Almighty Buck

Money may not be the only reason that you have decided to start up a small business. In fact, entrepreneurs tend to have an inborn need to create and build empires that reflect who they are and that can be passed on to future generations. But starting and managing a business is a risky venture and with risk comes the opportunity for reward.

Conventional wisdom says that you should sacrifice short-term monetary rewards for long-term gain. Many small-business owners not only do not think about getting a return on the money they have invested into their business, they don't even take a salary for the labor they invest. "I'll start taking a salary later when the business can afford it," is a refrain I frequently hear from small-business owners just starting out.

The danger of this thinking is that you may simply be subsidizing a business that cannot survive without you working and investing for free. The only successful business model is one that is able to pay all of its expenses as well as provide a return to its investors. Think about how long Microsoft would last if it couldn't pay its managers or pay dividends on its shares. Likewise, for your business to be successful, it will ultimately have to pay a manager, whether it's you or someone that you hire for the position.

Plan your remuneration right from the beginning. You know how much you will need from the business to pay your current expenses and you know how much you will have to set aside every year to fund your retirement (see Chapter 4). This is the minimum remuneration that you will need to plan for. If your business will not have access to the external financing necessary to pay you as the manager, make sure that you know how long it will be before it is able to do so. For example, it is easier to forego a salary if you know that, in six months, the business will start paying you one. This will also help with your own personal financial planning.

The bottom line is, even if money is not your primary motivation for starting your business, plan for profits and build your business model around profitability. Not only will it make your life more comfortable now, but it will increase the value of your business when it comes time to sell it or pass it on to the next generation (we'll talk more about exiting your business later in the chapter).

What Is the Purpose of Your Business?

The first step in planning your new business is to define what your business actually is. What will it provide to its customers? For example, if you want to open a hair salon, you must first define the range of services it will provide. Will it simply provide haircuts? Or will it be a full-service spa with high-end services like massage and facials?

The next planning step is to define your market. Who will your customers be? This will help you to target your marketing and promotions to be able to get at your potential customer base. This planning step will require some analysis. You need to make sure that the people you are targeting would really purchase your product or service. For example, if you have a car dealership that sells BMWs, you would more likely target wealthy business owners than penniless students. This may be a new concept for you if you have never run a business before and you may feel uncomfortable making generalizations about people based on their income or social stature. But you are simply trying to identify the group of consumers who are most likely to be interested in what you have to sell.

The third planning step is to identify where you want to be in your industry. If you are a massage therapist, do you want to be the least expensive? Be the most knowledgeable? Have the most flexible hours? This information will translate into your vision statement for your business: an all-encompassing statement about what your business stands for and what its mandate is. For a fuller discussion of developing a vision statement for your business, please refer to the third book in the *Numbers 101 for Small Business* series, *Managing Business Growth*.

Once you have decided on the overall direction of your new business, it's time to start the detailed planning process.

The Business Plan

Every small-business owner is told to write a business plan before starting a small business. But what is a business plan really and who is it for?

Many small-business owners prepare a business plan solely because their bank demands that they do. They find a template online and fill in the blanks. Once the bank has reviewed it (or tucked it into a file without looking at it, as is often the case), the business owner never looks at it again and it collects dust on a shelf.

A business plan should, however, be a living, breathing, ever-changing document. It is the guidebook for your business to follow. It is to your business what the Constitution is to the United States: a set of guiding principles and the road map to get there. Remember, though, that the road map for your business will be constantly changing as you meet challenges in your business's operating environment and as you make changes to take advantage of new opportunities in the market. You will frequently review and update your business plan and compare your actual results to your plans.

The primary user of the business plan should be you, the owner. However, there will be many other potential users of your business plan, including:

- **Lenders.** They will want to make sure that they are lending money to a solid enterprise that has a probability of success.

- **Key employees.** When you hire a manager or other employee critical to the success of your business, you will want to make sure that he or she knows the business plan and will manage the business accordingly.

- **Investors.** Venture capitalists and other potential investors will want to ensure that their money will be well invested.

- **Customers.** There may be times where securing a large contract means providing background material on your business and the business plan is an important document in that context.

- **Potential merger partners or acquisition targets.** If you are proposing to merge with or buy another company, the owners of that company will want to make certain that your business is both financially and philosophically sound.

What Should My Business Plan Include?

Your business plan should be detailed enough so that readers can understand what the business does and how it will go about doing it, but not too long or detailed that they will get lost in the minutia.

There are as many opinions on what should be included in a business plan as there are advisers, but Sample 5 is an example of critical information that should be included. Note also that you may alter your basic business plan depending on the reader. For example, a bank may be interested in very different information than a key employee. Be prepared to tailor your plan to different groups of readers.

SAMPLE 5
BUSINESS PLAN OUTLINE

BUSINESS PLAN OUTLINE

I. **EXECUTIVE SUMMARY**
   1. Overall purpose of the business
   2. The competition and the business's place in the industry
   3. The market
   4. Growth strategy
   5. Profitability and projections
   6. Human resources
   7. Financing structure and requirements

II. **EXTERNAL ENVIRONMENT AND INDUSTRY ANALYSIS**
   1. Geographical operating environment and constraints
   2. The industry
   3. Product or service analysis
   4. Development and operating strategy

III. **THE MARKET**
   1. Market size in the geographical operating environment
   2. Competitive analysis of market servicing
   3. Customer group profile
   4. Market share growth strategy

IV. **OPERATIONAL MANAGEMENT**
   1. Cash flow projections: 12 months and 5 years
   2. Break-even and capacity analysis
   3. Cost structure of business
   4. Profitability potential and timing
   5. Operating location and warehousing
   6. Operating cycle
   7. Life cycle timing

SAMPLE 5 — Continued

V. MARKETING AND PROMOTION
1. Competitive strategy
2. Sales strategies and outlets
3. Pricing analysis
4. Advertising strategy
5. Product distribution or service provision
6. Servicing

VI. GROWTH STRATEGY
1. Overall growth strategy
2. Financing plan
3. Growth limitations and constraints
4. External and internal challenges and obstacles
5. New product or service development and introduction
6. Exit and harvest strategies

VII. HUMAN RESOURCES
1. Organizational structure
2. Key employee profiles
3. Ownership and investment structure
4. Remuneration and performance evaluation
5. Governance
6. External advisory team

VIII. FINANCING REQUIREMENTS
1. Amount and use of required funds
2. Current debt/equity structure
3. Proposed return on funds

IX. HISTORICAL FINANCIAL INFORMATION (when available)
1. Balance sheet
2. Income statement
3. Statement of cash flows
4. Ratio analysis

At first, the sheer volume of the information required for this document may overwhelm you, but take it one piece at a time. All of this information should be thought about and planned out before you open your doors. It may take several months for you to gather and plan the information. The more upfront planning you do, however, the more probability of success you will have.

The Monthly Management Operating Plan

Once you have mapped out the overall direction and strategy that your business will take in your business plan, it's time to start looking at how you will manage the ongoing operations. How will you know if your revenues are on track? Will you have enough money next month to pay your suppliers? All these questions are answered in the monthly management operating plan (or the MMOP). The MMOP allows you to regularly monitor the operations of your business. It will tell you instantly if you are on track with your profit projections or if your liquidity is less than planned. Your MMOP should contain the following information:

- A monthly budget showing actual-versus-planned figures
- A monthly cash flow statement showing actual-versus-planned figures
- Ratio analysis, including turnover and capital ratios
- An analysis of all actual key performance indicators compared to the plan
- A synopsis of the external and internal business environment and how it has affected the business
- A thorough analysis of employee productivity
- A summary of promotional efforts and their measurable impact on results

Your monthly management operating plan should give you an analysis at a glance. In the beginning when you are the only employee in the business, you will be pulling this information yourself from your bookkeeping system, updating the plan, and then reviewing the results. As you grow, you will simply be reviewing the results and others will be doing the mechanical gathering. For a more detailed discussion of the MMOP and how to calculate ratios and develop key performance indicators, please refer to the second book in the *Numbers 101 for Small Business* series, *Financial Management 101.*

Your Exit Strategy

It may seem strange to talk about getting out of your business before you've even gotten into it, but you should plan your leave-taking right from the beginning. The main reason for this is that you never know when you will be leaving. Even if you plan on running your business literally until you drop, that day may come sooner than you're expecting and your heirs will be left with the task of harvesting the value that you have built up in your business. Another reason for planning your leave is to make sure that your business is always working in concert with your retirement goals. If you expect to make a $100,000 gain on the sale of your business to help fund your retirement, you need to plan the growth that will be required for that gain right from the beginning. Your exit strategy will be included as a part of your business plan and may change over time as the external environment and your business goals change.

Chapter Summary

➡ A successful business model is able to pay all the expenses of the business and a return to the investors, so planning for your own remuneration and profit is important.

➡ Your business planning should start with your overall vision for the business, whom it will serve, and how it will operate.

➡ Your business plan is a living, breathing, ever-changing document that guides your business operations and growth adhering to its underlying principles.

➡ The monthly management operating plan compares your actual operating results to your plans to make sure that you're on track.

Chapter
6

Putting Your Money Where Your Business Plan Is

A look at capitalizing your business. How much money will you need? Where will it come from? How expensive is it going to be?

Introduction

A business can only grow as fast as its capital allows. Capital can come from three sources, either solely, or a combination of the three:

- Your own resources
- Resources of an external investor
- Revenue generated from your business

Eventually, internally generated revenue will provide the operating capital for the business. Profits will be plowed back in to the business to allow it to keep a war chest or savings for the bad times or to finance further growth and expansion. In the beginning, however, you will have to rely on your own resources or those of an external investor.

CASE STUDY

Craig had now met with his partner, Gordon, for the visioning session and had prepared the initial business plan for EarthPower. Both partners were excited about the new venture and had created a list of potential investors and lenders. They had determined that they needed at least $195,000 to get started, which would pay for their start-up expenses as well as the first nine months of operations, when their projected expenses would be more than their revenues.

The partners decided to meet with their bankers first to find out the bank's position on funding their venture. Gordon also wanted the two to meet with a private investor who provided investment funds to new companies that provide alternative energy solutions.

Before meeting with potential lenders, Craig and Gordon met with Vivian again to work on their presentation. They knew that they would only have one opportunity to present themselves and their new company to lenders. They needed to think about and have answers to the questions that lenders would ask them. They also needed to have well-thought out cash flow projections based on conservative estimates of the business's growth and revenue patterns.

Once the partners worked out all the bugs in their presentation, they approached their respective banks to see if they could get debt financing. Craig's bank declined to offer financing as the venture was too new and did not have a financial track record. Gordon's bank, however, was willing to lend them $125,000 at 7 percent in exchange for a general security agreement, which meant that the bank was using the assets of the business as collateral for the

It's important that, as part of your business plan, you identify and quantify your financing needs. You will need cash for some or all of these reasons:

- **Start-up costs.** Your initial investment into the business might include inventory, equipment purchases, rental deposits, and legal and accounting fees.
- **Shortfalls of revenues over expenses.** You will still need to pay your suppliers and pay the fixed costs of running the business even before you become profitable.
- **War chest.** This is simply a fund of money (or short-term investments) set aside for a rainy day or for taking advantage of sudden opportunities.
- **Capital equipment replacement.** Eventually, your equipment will break down or become obsolete and you will have to re-invest in new equipment.
- **Growth.** Expansion of your current operations may mean additional costs related to advertising, payroll, warehousing, or product research and development. You will likely incur these costs before you generate the revenues as a result of the expansion.

Let's have a look at how to project your need for capital.

Projecting Your Funding Needs

The process of raising cash is not limited to starting up your business. You will have ongoing need for capital in all stages of your business. Financing needs to be an integrated part of your ongoing operational and strategic management.

In the start-up phase, however, you have two initial concerns:

1. Paying for the start-up costs
2. Providing liquidity to the business until the revenues can sustain it

Paying for the start-up costs

When outlining your necessary start-up costs, take your time and ensure that you are capturing all the costs that there are. You may forget seemingly insignificant things that can add up to you shelling out several more thousand dollars upfront than you expected. Typical start-up costs include the following:

- **Purchase of initial inventory.** This will clearly be more important for a retail operation or manufacturer.

- **Capital equipment.** Not only will you have to buy any equipment that you need to make the product or provide the service, but you may need peripheral equipment like vehicles, computers, and office furniture.

- **Rental deposits.** You may have to pay a deposit on your rented location or on any rented office equipment.

- **Supplies.** Although items like pens, paper, and staplers don't seem significant, the initial cost of stocking your office can be high.

- **Insurance premiums.** Although you may pay monthly premiums in the future for liability or business insurance, your carrier may require that you pay the first year upfront.

- **Professional fees.** You may incur legal and accounting fees to set up your business and also to retain advice on planning and strategizing.

- **Renovation costs.** You may need to design and build or renovate your interior office or store space. Costs can include designing, carpentry, painting, carpet, sound systems, and a host of other expenses.

- **Delay costs.** This is an expense that smart entrepreneurs factor into their calculations. If you can't open your doors on time because the space isn't ready or the product isn't available, you will still be incurring all of the operational costs of running the business without the revenues that you had planned.

Once you have outlined and valued all your projected start-up costs, build in a cushion, anywhere from 5 percent to 10 percent of your total costs, to give you some breathing room in case of cost overruns.

Providing liquidity to the business

The second requirement for cash will come from the cash flow projections you have prepared as part of your business plan. Whenever your projected cash balance falls below zero, you have a shortfall that you will have to finance. For example, if you are expecting cash shortfalls in the first three months of $5,000, $3,200, and $1,450 respectively before you start generating net cash surpluses, you will need to find $9,650 in funding for the shortfalls. Once again, build in a cushion in case your shortfalls exceed those planned.

CASE STUDY
continued

loan. Craig and Gordon then approached the private investor who offered to put up the final $70,000 in exchange for a 10 percent ownership stake in the company. The partners discussed the offer extensively before finally deciding that giving away a small piece of the company was a fair price to pay for the needed financing.

They were finally ready to prepare for the start up of their new business.

Let's have a closer look at putting together your cash flow projection. Sample 6 is an example of a cash flow projection that has been reproduced from the second book in the *Numbers 101 for Small Business* series, *Financial Management 101.* There are several important things to note as you are preparing your own cash flow projection:

1. Keep in mind the difference between cash flows and revenues and expenses. Cash flow refers to the actual inflows and outflows of cash, whereas revenues and expenses (as reported on the income statement) can reflect items where the cash transaction hasn't yet occurred. For example, if you sell an item today but your customer won't pay you for 30 days, this will show up on an income statement as a revenue item, but would not show up in a cash flow report because you haven't received the money yet. The cash flow projection deals only with actual inflows and outflows of money. Its purpose is to make sure that you don't run out of money.

2. The "Cash receipts" line reflects your estimate of the actual receipt of accounts receivable, not your sales projections. For example, you may collect only 15 percent of your revenues in the month of sale, 63 percent the following month, 18 percent in two months, and 4 percent in three months. Sample 7 is an example of what that might look like.

Notice that although you are reporting $1,250 in sales for the month of January, your cash flow report would only show cash receipts of $187.50. Make sure when you are preparing your cash flow projection that you take into consideration the average length of time it will take to collect your receivables.

3. All cash receipts and cash payments appear on the cash flow projection, regardless of their source. In the example, there is a line for the purchase of capital equipment. This item would not be recorded on the income statement (it is a balance sheet item) but it is a payment of cash. Any projected purchases such as equipment and inventory should be included in your projection. The same would be true of proceeds from a new loan. If the bank lends you $25,000, it would show as a receipt of cash on the cash flow report.

4. If the closing cash balance on the cash flow projection falls below zero at the end of any month, you will have to consider how to finance the shortfall. It is okay to have a net

Sample 6
CASH FLOW REPORT

Small Company Inc.
Cash flow report
January – December 2004

	Jan	Feb	Mar	Apr	May	Jun	Jul	Aug	Sep	Oct	Nov	Dec	Total
Cash receipts	3,725	4,612	4,109	3,289	5,085	5,139	4,103	3,578	3,945	4,210	6,412	5,303	53,510
Cost of goods sold	1,895	2,416	1,989	1,675	2,756	2,708	1,965	1,792	2,006	2,165	3,260	2,585	27,212
Advertising	50	50	50	50	50	50	103	50	50	50	50	50	653
Bank charges	7	7	7	7	7	7	7	7	7	7	7	17	94
Office expenses	61	68	66	72	69	65	73	57	53	65	76	71	796
Professional fees	-	-	-	412	-	-	-	-	-	-	-	-	412
Supplies	39	31	42	19	65	58	17	39	42	58	63	51	524
Telephone and utilities	87	89	79	96	85	89	97	89	71	69	59	76	986
Vehicle expenses	39	47	32	45	49	51	34	31	32	41	39	38	478
Wages	306	310	285	296	314	312	342	284	292	325	312	295	3,673
Purchase of capital equipment	-	-		1,953	-	475	-	-	-	710	-	-	3,138
Net cash inflow (outflow)	1,241	1,594	1,559	(1,336)	1,690	1,324	1,465	1,229	1,392	720	2,546	2,120	15,544
Opening cash	1,259	2,500	4,094	5,653	4,317	6,007	7,331	8,796	10,025	11,417	12,137	14,683	
Closing cash	2,500	4,094	5,653	4,317	6,007	7,331	8,796	10,025	11,417	12,137	14,683	16,803	

SAMPLE 7
CASH INFLOWS

		Jan	Feb	Mar	Apr	May
Revenue		1,250.00	1,095.00	2,470.00	1,750.00	975.00
Collected:						
	Current (15%)	187.50	164.25	370.50	262.50	146.25
	Next month (63%)		787.50	689.85	1,556.10	1,102.50
	2 months (18%)			225.00	197.10	444.60
	3 months (4%)				50.00	43.80
Totals					**2,065.70**	**1,737.15**

cash outflow in any particular month (as in the month of April in the example) as long as there is a cumulative cash surplus going into the month. This would roughly translate to a positive projected balance in the business bank account, which would be able to absorb any shortfall up to that balance. It is only when the cumulative balance drops below zero (i.e., you have no money in the bank account) that you have to have other financing in place.

To brush up on bookkeeping basics, take a look at *Bookkeepers' Boot Camp*, the first book in the *Numbers 101 for Small Business* series.

Sources of Funding

Because funding in the start-up period is not likely to come from net profits right away, you must look to either your own resources or those of other lenders or investors.

Your own resources could include:

- Savings
- Personal loan or line of credit
- Re-mortgage of your house
- Credit cards
- Borrowings from family or friends

Some of these sources are preferable to others. We will discuss these in more detail in the next chapter.

Other lender or investor funds could include:

- Business bank loans

- Business lines of credit
- Business credit cards
- Private loans
- Leaseback agreements
- Business property mortgages
- Stock sales (in the case of corporations)
- Venture capitalists
- Joint venture partnerships

As with personal borrowing, some types of business borrowings are preferable to others and will be discussed in the following two chapters. Some of these sources of funding represent equity, or ownership, stakes in the business, while others represent debt to outside parties. The type of borrowing may have an effect on the debt to equity ratio of the business, which may impact the ability of the business to borrow further funds.

A Bank's Perspective

Let's have a look at financing from the bank's perspective. This will be a useful viewpoint to keep in mind as you are preparing to see your banker.

You are the bank manager at a small regional bank. Tony has called you this morning and has set up an appointment to see you at two o'clock this afternoon. Tony and his wife have been personal banking clients at your bank for over ten years. Tony has been a mechanic at the local car dealership for as long as you have known him. Today on the telephone, he has told you briefly about his plan to start his own auto repair shop. He is coming to you today to discuss financing the new business. As a bank manager entrusted with the safety of the bank's money, what are the most important considerations you will have when deciding whether Tony gets the funding? Clearly, you will be concerned with his ability to make the loan payments. In order to make the loan payments, Tony will have to make enough money in his new business to cover them off. He will be quitting his job to start the business and his wife stays at home with the household and children, so his only source of income will be the new business.

The second thing that you will consider is how to protect the bank's interests if the business is not as successful as planned and Tony defaults on the payments. The bank will want to be able to use some of Tony's other assets to settle the outstanding debt so that the bank is not out of pocket for the remaining balance of the loan.

In order to get comfort on both of those issues, there are a number of things that you will be looking for Tony to be able to demonstrate to you when he comes to see you this afternoon:

- **Is the business built on a solid plan?** How much "homework" has Tony done to prove that this is a viable business venture?

- **Does he have enough entrepreneurial skills to build and manage a business?** Tony has indicated that he will be responsible for the ongoing management of the operation, so you will need some idea as to whether he has any training or ability in finance, bookkeeping, operational management, strategic planning, and human resource management.

- **Is the business built on a model that will have sufficient cash flow to pay its creditors, including your bank?** As a bank manager, you have to be concerned not only with your bank's exposure to Tony's risk of failure, but the exposure of other lenders. For example, if Tony is able to make your bank's loan payments but defaults on the mortgage on the repair shop, the mortgage lender can foreclose on the property, leaving Tony without a business or source of income.

- **Does Tony have enough assets to satisfy the outstanding amount of the loan if he defaults on the payments?** The last thing that you want is to have Tony not make his payments and the bank having to seize assets, but you certainly want to have that option open to you as a last resort.

These are the major concerns of any lender. Keep these in mind when you prepare your business plan and when you see your banker. Make sure that you have the answers to the questions that he or she is most likely to ask. For more information on getting a loan from a bank, check out *Financial Management 101,* the second book in the *Numbers 101 for Small Business* series.

Chapter Summary

➡ During the start-up phase, your business will most likely need financing from your own personal resources or from an outside lender.

➡ You will need to finance your start-up expenses and any shortfall in revenues over expenses until your business begins to turn a profit.

➡ External financing can come from one or more of a number of sources, including banks, venture capitalists, investors, and private lenders.

➡ Prepare answers ahead of time to address the most likely questions that your banker (or other lenders) will ask you when you seek financing.

Chapter
7

Debt Financing

Debt is a common source of funding a business. In this chapter we examine the pros and cons of borrowing.

Introduction

Once you have determined the dollar amount of capital that you need to fund the start-up phase of your business, it's time to start evaluating the potential sources of financing. In this chapter, we will look at debt financing. In the next, we will examine sources of equity financing.

Debt financing can take many forms but it basically means that a lender has loaned you funds that you are obligated to repay in the future. Debt financing doesn't involve an ownership stake in the business, but simply a promise to pay. That promise can take several forms, depending on the financing tool and the guarantees involved.

When considering debt financing, *who* you are borrowing from is just as important as *what* you are borrowing. An experienced lender, such as a bank or a venture capitalist, can assist with advice as well as money, whereas borrowing from friends or relatives can often cause more headaches than it solves if they choose to interfere in business affairs.

Another important consideration is the term of financing. You may need to borrow capital to pay for the land and building upon which you operate. These are long-term assets and should be backed with long-term financing. Think of what would happen if you took out a two-year term loan on the property and couldn't refinance at the end of two years. Make sure that the term of the financing matches the term of the underlying assets.

Let's look at some of the more common forms of debt financing and their characteristics.

Your Own Resources

This is the first place you should start for many reasons. First, using your own funds is the least risky proposition from an asset seizure point of view. You (the lender or investor) are not likely to foreclose on you (the borrower). Second, external lenders will want to see that you have funds at risk, that is to say that you believe enough in your venture to put your own hard-earned cash into it. If you want the external lenders to risk their capital, you should have something at stake as well.

You may have to save for a considerable amount of time to start your own business. Other financing may be scarce in the beginning and the more of your own savings you have, the better the likelihood of financial stability and growth.

It is important to remember, however, that, just as you wouldn't invest all of your life's savings in a single stock, you shouldn't put all of your eggs in the same basket by dumping it all into your business. Make sure that you have a number of savings vehicles for the future.

Credit Cards

Just as in your personal financial life, credit cards can be a dangerous source of business financing. Many entrepreneurs have run up their cards to the limit to generate the start-up capital needed for their business. This generally happens when a small-business owner doesn't qualify for bank financing.

The problems with credit cards are many. First, the interest rate tends to be exorbitant. Credit card rates do not tend to move with changes in market interest rates, so even when other rates are low, credit card rates can be upwards of 20 percent per annum. Second, if you do not qualify for bank financing in the first place, running up a high balance on your credit cards will more than likely guarantee that the banks will look even more unfavorably on you in the future.

It may be tempting to be overly optimistic and think that you will be able to pay down the credit cards quickly but you must remember that there are many uncontrollable variables in starting a business that may require more capital than you expected.

Bottom line: Try to avoid credit cards as much as possible. If you do use them for starting up your business, make sure that you pay them off as quickly as possible. Also, make sure that you at least pay the minimum amounts required and pay them on time; late credit card payments show up on your credit rating.

Suppliers

Suppliers are often a much-overlooked source of financing for a new business. Most suppliers offer credit terms on purchases, ranging anywhere from 15 to 90 days on average. If you take advantage of your suppliers' credit terms, make sure that payments are made on time. Suppliers can charge a late payment penalty that can be higher than credit card rates.

Some suppliers offer an early payment discount that can equate to a very large savings. For example, if a supplier offers 2/10 net 30 terms, this means that you get an early payment discount of 2 percent if the bill is paid in 10 days; otherwise it's due in 30 days. If, for example, your purchase was for $1,000, you would only have to pay $980 if you pay within 10 days. Another way to look at it is to say that 2 percent will buy you an extra 20 days of credit. But how much does that credit really cost?

By not taking the discount, you are borrowing $980 for an extra 20 days and paying $20 for that privilege ($1,000 minus $980). The interest rate for the period is 2.04 percent ($20 / $980 = 2.04%).

There are 18.25 20-day periods in the year (365 / 20). The effective annual rate (EAR) is calculated as:

$$EAR = (1+0.0204)^{18.25} - 1 = 44.6\%$$

You are essentially paying an interest rate of 44.6 percent to borrow the funds for an extra 20 days. That's pretty expensive credit! Another way to look at it is to say that you are making 44.6 percent on your money by taking the discount.

On the other end of the spectrum, many suppliers charge interest on overdue accounts. A common term of sale is 2 percent interest per month for each month overdue. What is the true cost of taking advantage of this form of financing? At first glance, it would appear to be 24 percent annually (2 percent X 12 months), but it is actually higher than that, due to the negative pull of compounding. The effective annual rate is actually:

$$EAR = (1+0.02)^{12} - 1 = 26.82\% \text{ annually}$$

It would therefore cost you 26.82 percent to use this source of financing beyond 30 days. That is higher than bank financing and even higher than most credit cards. You must weigh this cost against the short-term cash flow benefit of using this source of financing.

Another issue to think about when deciding if you will pay later than stipulated by the supplier is the impact on your credit rating with that supplier. Getting an extra 20 days of credit might not be worth having the supplier put you on a cash-only basis in the future because you don't pay on time.

Bottom line: Use your suppliers' credit terms but beware the cost (in terms of dollars and credit history) of not paying them on time.

Friends and Family

Your friends and family may have many different reasons for wanting to lend money to your new business. They may want to help you out by giving you that little boost when you're first starting out. They may be shrewd investors, knowing that you'll walk barefoot over broken glass to pay them back.

As we have discussed previously, it may be very difficult for you to attract outside capital before you have established a track record. Friends and family may be your only option for a while. Before you borrow from people you know, take the following into consideration:

- Make certain that your understanding of the arrangement is the same as that of the lender and that you have thoroughly discussed all aspects of the proposed loan.
- Fully document the loan just as the bank would if the bank were lending to you. Spell out the term, interest rate, repayment terms, and any security that may be pledged against the loan. Have both parties sign a copy of the loan agreement.

- Treat the loan as a business arrangement. Be sure that you make repayments on time and that you don't let things "slide" because it's someone you know.

- Make sure that the loan is handled properly from a tax perspective. In many jurisdictions, you will not be able to deduct the interest that you pay on the loan for tax purposes if the lender does not claim the interest income. This could significantly raise your effective cost of borrowing. Discuss the proposed loan with your accountant before signing.

Bottom line: Proceed with caution when borrowing from friends and family and make sure that the arrangement is well documented and formalized.

Banks

Banks can assist you with many different types of financing and will most likely be one of the cornerstones of your business. Banks can provide:

- Lines of credit

- Unsecured loans

- Receivables financing

- Loans secured by property or equipment

- Loans secured by the owner's personal guarantee (and assets)

- Mortgage financing

As discussed in the previous chapter, make sure that you have thoroughly thought through your financing needs before you see your banker, so that you can be clear about what type of financing you are seeking.

Banks will be very interested in what types of assets (personal and business) you have with which they can secure the loan, especially when you are just starting out and do not yet have a financial history. Loans that are secured with assets will generally be at a lower interest rate than unsecured loans. However, if you default on a secured loan, you will risk losing the asset that backs the loan. If that asset is your residence, you risk homelessness. Always make sure that you understand what assets you are risking when signing a bank loan.

Banks may also have other stipulations when lending to your small business, including required liquidity ratios and restrictions on other debt. If your business fails to meet these requirements at any time over the course of the loan (called "going offside"), the bank can call the loan and you may find yourself scrambling for another quick source of funds.

Table 1 provides a summary of financial ratios. For a more detailed discussion of ratios, please refer to *Financial Management 101*, the second book in the *Numbers 101 for Small Business* series.

Bottom line: Bank financing may be difficult to get in the start-up period and may have many restrictions attached to it. However, it is a lower cost financing solution that forms the basis of most small business funding.

Leasing Companies

Leasing companies specialize in financing manufacturing or office equipment. You may find that the company that you purchase the equipment from has its own leasing arm and can handle the entire transaction for you.

Equipment leases are always secured by the equipment being leased, so if you fall behind on your payments, you risk losing the equipment. On the other hand, the interest rates tend to be low on this type of finance both because of its secured nature and also because the leasing company may be using the lease as a purchase incentive.

It can sometimes be difficult to ascertain the effective interest rate on a lease so always make sure you thoroughly read the documents and discuss any questions with your accountant. Knowing, for example, that you will pay $450 per month for 60 months tells you nothing about the rate of interest you are paying. Repairs and maintenance is another area that you need to be clear on. Who is responsible if the equipment breaks down during the term of the lease: you or the leasing company? Also, make sure that you understand what happens at the end of the term. Some leases simply turn the ownership over to you at that point. Others require a buy-out and you will need to figure that into your calculations.

Bottom line: Leasing can be a great way to finance equipment purchases, but it's important to make sure that you understand exactly what you're paying.

Private Lenders

Like banks, private lending is used in many different applications. The most common, however, is borrowing from a private lender because you have been turned down for other types of financing.

TABLE 1
A QUICK REFERENCE TO RATIOS

Solvency or liquidity ratios

    1. Current ratio = Current assets/Current liabilities

    Am I going to be able to pay my short-term debts?

    2. Total debt ratio = Total debt/Total assets

    How much leverage do I have?

Asset and debt management ratios

    3. Inventory turnover = COGS/Inventory

    How long before I sell my product?

    4. Receivables turnover = Sales/Accounts receivable

    How long before I get paid for what I sell?

    5. Payables turnover = COGS/Accounts payable

    How quickly do I pay my suppliers?

    6. Times interest earned = EBIT/Interest expense

    Do I have enough income to pay the interest on my debt?

Profitability ratios

    7. Profit margin = Net income/Sales

    How efficiently am I managing my expenses?

    8. Return on assets = Net profit/Total assets

    How well am I using my assets to generate profit?

    9. Return on investment = Normalized net income/money invested

    What kind of return am I getting on the money I've put into the business?

Because of the increased risk to the lender (who would definitely know that the bank wouldn't deal with you), the interest rates charged in these types of situations tend to be high.

There are private lenders, sometimes referred to as "angel investors," who enjoy the financial risk and the accompanying thrill of helping a new business to get off the ground. These lenders can be difficult to find, but speak with your lawyer, accountant, or financial planner about whether they have the appropriate contacts.

The biggest danger with using a private lender is hidden fees. In some cases there are none, but make sure that you read through the entire agreement (and it's generally a good idea to let your lawyer review the document as well) before you sign anything. You should understand all aspects of the loan, including interest rate, repayment terms, initial or renewal fees, assets secured, and fees charged for missed or bounced payments.

Bottom line: Private lenders may be your source of last resort but make sure you understand the whole picture.

Chapter Summary

➡ Debt financing involves borrowing funds and repaying them over time, with interest, to the lender.

➡ Loans that are secured with equipment, real estate, or other assets tend to have lower interest rates than unsecured loans.

➡ You should look to your own savings first as your best source of funds.

➡ When borrowing from outside sources, make sure you understand the whole agreement before signing.

Chapter
8

Equity Financing

Another source of funds is through the sale of ownership in the business. We look at the major considerations in this chapter.

Introduction

Another potential source of financing is equity financing. Equity financing differs from debt financing in a few key ways. It usually involves a longer term investment than debt financing. As the recipient of the funds, you will pay a return to the investor, usually in the form of dividends. You generally do not pay back the original investment unless the investor wants to "cash out."

Equity financing also generally involves two other features: ownership share and profit participation. When an investor takes an equity stake in your business, he or she is buying a slice of the pie. You are transferring some of the risks and rewards of ownership of your business over to the investor. Because the risk to the investor is greater than in a loan situation, the investor will expect a higher return in the form of dividends. Dividends may be a fixed payment (similar to a loan's interest rate) or may be a percentage of the after-tax net profits of the business, depending on the type of investment. We will look at the common types of equity investments in more detail later in the chapter.

Finding people willing to invest in your start-up business for the long term may be quite difficult. Your business does not yet have an established financial track record and the risks may outstrip the appetites of many potential investors. Start-up businesses tend to have more debt financing in the beginning stages and then slowly convert towards more equity financing as the business reaches the maturity stage of its life cycle (for a more in-depth discussion of the life cycle of a business, please refer to the third book in the *Numbers 101 for Small Business* series, *Managing Business Growth*).

Let's take a look at the characteristics of some of the more common types of equity investments.

Common Shares

Common shareholders are the owners of a corporation. For example, if you own 50 percent of the common shares of a corporation, you own 50 percent of the business. The dividends paid to the common shareholders are set by the board of directors and are equal in proportion to the shareholdings. In a small incorporated corporation, you are most likely the president and you would, therefore, decide what dividends are to be paid out to the common shareholders (a group of which you are likely a member as well).

Common shareholders also have voting rights in the corporation. If you have sold, for example, 55 percent of the common shares of your corporation, those shares can control the vote. You may find yourself without any way to influence the decision making in your own business. Even if the minority shareholders own less than 50 percent, they can still meddle in the affairs of the business and slow down its operations or growth.

When a corporation winds up, it pays its liabilities from its assets. Whatever is left (if anything) goes to the common shareholders. If that company is insolvent (one of the main reasons for wind up), the investors may not be able to recover their original investment.

Because dividend payments are out of the control of the investors and because of the risk of loss of the original investment, it is unlikely that you will be able to attract common shareholders in your start-up business; however, you may wish to pursue this type of financing as you grow.

Preferred Shares

Preferred share arrangements come in all colors and stripes. Although preferred shares still represent an ownership stake in the corporation, they frequently are stripped of their voting and profit participation rights. In exchange for giving up those rights, preferred shareholders receive a higher ranking on the list of payouts when the company winds up. In other words, preferred shareholders will be paid before common shareholders.

Another common feature of preferred shares is a fixed dividend rate. Instead of having to wait and see if there's any profit to distribute, preferred shares may be paid, for example, a 6 percent fixed dividend. This dividend payment would also rank higher than any potential dividend payments to the common shareholders. As the value of the dividend is fixed, when interest rates fall in the market place, these shares become more valuable and can be sold for a gain above what was originally invested.

Partnership

A partnership is a non-incorporated company owned by two or more individuals or corporations. Each partner would have an equity statement showing his or her original investment, the accumulated net income accruing to each partner, the draws that have been taken against that income, and the ending equity balance. Table 2 is an example of an equity statement for a 50/50 partnership.

Note how each partner has contributed the same amount of capital and that the income over the years has been split 50/50 in accordance with the partnership percentages. Joe and Melissa may choose to withdraw this fund of capital at a different rate, depending on the need for money and tax considerations. So, it is quite possible that partners may have different net equity positions at any point in time.

When the partnership winds up, the partners will split whatever is left over after the liabilities are satisfied with the assets based on their equity positions. It is hoped that they will be able to receive the dollar amount of their net equity positions, but, for example, if there was only $71,050 left to distribute back to the partners, Joe would get $17,413 (45,410/185,290 X 71,050) and Melissa would get $53,637 (139,880/185,290 X 71,050).

You may choose to bring partners on board to finance your start-up or expansion. Keep in mind that partners will most likely want to have a say in the business's operations. Make sure that the

TABLE 2
EQUITY STATEMENT FOR A 50/50 PARTNERSHIP

	Joe	Melissa	Total
Original investment	$43,000	$43,000	$86,000
Cumulative profit	129,000	129,000	258,000
Current year profit	30,410	30,410	60,820
Draws	(157,000)	(62,530)	219,530
Net equity	$45,410	$139,880	$185,290

partnership agreement has had every facet spelled out in detail, including how decisions are made. Each partner's lawyer should review the document before signing to make sure that nothing has been overlooked.

It's very tempting on start-up to partner with someone. You both have vision for the company and have a very rosy outlook on its chances. It is at this point that a partnership agreement should be signed. Down the road, if there are disagreements, the partnership agreement should spell out how the impasse is handled. Signed agreements make good partners!

Joint Ventures

A joint venture in its simplest sense is a short-term partnership. Let's say that you own a business that is a wholesaler of sporting goods. That means that you purchase the goods from the manufacturer and sell to retail stores. You have run across an unusual situation that can be very profitable. One of the manufacturers that you deal with has a surplus of 75,000 trail bikes. The manufacturer is willing to sell the whole lot to you for $57 a piece, for a total of $4,275,000. You are certain that you can sell these to retailers in a short period of time and make a substantial profit. The only problem is that you don't have over four million dollars lying around. You would then look for a joint venture partner: someone who is willing to put up the money in order to split the profits on the sale.

Joint ventures are a win-win situation. They differ from partnerships in that they relate to very specific activities. Each joint venturer, whether it's an individual or a company, may have other business operations on his or her own.

Forming a joint venture can be a great way of taking advantage of opportunities that cross your path as you grow your business, but, like every other type of joint ownership arrangement, it's important to map out everything in a signed agreement before starting the project.

Venture Capitalists

Venture capitalists are a unique breed. They seek out businesses that they feel have tremendous opportunities for growth and profit. Then they invest funds in these businesses and harvest a piece of the profit at a later date. There are several considerations for you to look at when deciding whether to approach a venture capitalist for financing:

- Venture capitalists usually only fund existing businesses that have a track record of stability and a future potential of large profits.

- Venture capitalists are very hands on. Most have extensive business or management experience and want to help to drive the direction of the company. This can be very beneficial if you are deficient in these skills, but can also cause friction.

- Venture capitalists are interested only in increasing the worth of their equity stake. To that end, they will position the company towards going public or selling out to a larger company. This is how they will get their reward in the end. You may find yourself ending up with very little say in the company.

- Venture capitalists can find new markets and new acquisition targets for your company that you may not have thought of or had access to.

Before you seek out a venture capitalist, make sure that your goals for your business will align with the goals of the investor. If the venture capitalist makes money, you make money. You get to go along for the ride. You just may not be in the driver's seat.

Chapter Summary

➡ Equity financing is more permanent than debt financing and involves giving up an ownership stake in your business in exchange for capital.

➡ Common and preferred shares represent the ownership of a corporation with different risks and rewards.

➡ Partnerships are long-term pairings of individuals or corporations for business purposes, while joint ventures are pairings for specific and finite projects.

➡ Venture capitalists invest in businesses with great profit and growth potential in exchange for operational control.

Risky Business: How to Assess Business Risk

D o you really know what's at stake in your business? We look at business risk, from the chance of losing your home to collection issues.

Introduction

No one likes to contemplate risk. If you're a small-business owner, you certainly don't want to think about your business as being risky. But entrepreneurs are notorious for two things: overestimating profit potential and underestimating risk.

Risk lurks in every situation where you are obligated to perform certain things even when the situation or business climate changes. The risk to you is that the business will lose assets and profit. It is certainly true that along with risk comes the potential for reward, which is one of the main reasons for starting your business in the first place. It is critical, though, to make sure that you have a handle on your exposure to the risks in your business, both those that exist naturally and those that exist because of how the business is being managed.

Let's have a look at some common risks that you may be exposed to in your business and how to minimize them.

CASE STUDY

Craig was learning quickly about managing a business. Vivian had educated him about some of the risks that businesses could face and helped him to recognize those specific risks that EarthPower would be susceptible to.

EarthPower's major problem was going to be its vulnerability to changes in foreign exchange rates between the US dollar and the euro. The company would be paying most of its bills (including its loan payments) in US dollars, but a large segment of its sales would be made from EarthPower's Brussels office. The European market for alternative energy products is larger than in North America due to government incentives and a firmer commitment to reductions in the use of fossil fuels.

The whole concept of foreign exchange risk was foreign to Craig. He had no idea what drove foreign currencies, how he could fix the problem, or even what the nature of the problem was. Vivian cautioned that whenever the US dollar strengthened against the euro, EarthPower's profit margin would shrink. Because there were going to be large dollar amounts involved, she recommended that Craig and his partner, Gordon, discuss hedging strategies with the company's bank to offset some of the risk. Craig slept better at night knowing that the fledgling company's profit margins would be preserved regardless of the direction of foreign exchange rates.

Secured Loans

In Chapter 7, we discussed how having your loan secured with business assets (be they equipment, vehicles, or real estate) would generally mean a lower interest rate than with an unsecured loan. The other side of that coin, however, is that if you default on the loan payments, the lender has a right to repossess (repo) the assets that secure the loan. For example, if you have purchased $100,000 worth of manufacturing equipment with bank financing but have not achieved the level of planned profitability and therefore have fallen behind on loan payments, the bank may take the equipment away and sell it to try to recoup the outstanding amount on the loan. It would be impossible for you to operate without equipment and you may be hard pressed to find anyone else willing to lend to you with your default history.

Minimize the risk of losing your secured assets by carefully monitoring your cash flows and ensuring that you make all payments on time and meet all terms of the loan.

Personal Guarantees

A lender may require the personal guarantee of the business owner when there are not enough business assets to secure the financing. A personal guarantee means that if the business defaults on its obligations, you will be on the hook for the repayment whether or not the business is a separate legal entity.

A lender may go further than a general personal guarantee and may secure the business loan directly with personal assets, including the equity in your home, vehicles, and investment portfolios. The lender may take these assets from you to satisfy the terms of the business loan if the repayment terms are not met. Having personal assets secured may also make it difficult for you to seek personal financing such as investment loans or house mortgages.

Minimize this risk by seeking the lowest rate financing that does not require personal guarantees. If it is impossible to avoid a personal guarantee, revisit the issue with your lender on a regular basis to see if the guarantee can be waived after some history of prompt payment.

Fixed Price Agreements

Fixed price agreements can protect your business from inflation and price changes if used properly but can dramatically increase your risk if handled improperly.

Let's look at an example. You own a transportation company and have negotiated an agreement with a large poultry farm to ship chickens across the country in the coming year at a set price per mile. After the agreement has been signed, the government institutes a new "road tax" that will charge vehicle owners six cents per mile driven to help pay for roads and policing. The cost of providing the transportation service to your customer has increased dramatically, but, because you signed a fixed price agreement with your customer, you are unable to pass that cost along and it will end up eroding your profit margin. This is an example of fixed price agreements working against you.

To minimize this risk, make sure that all agreements signed with customers have a clause allowing for increases in pricing due to factors beyond your control.

Interest Rate Risk

You are exposed to interest rate risk when you have financing with an interest rate that changes with changing market conditions, also called floating rate interest. For example, if you have a $100,000 operating loan with the bank at a floating interest rate currently at 7.5 percent, you will be paying $7,500 in interest a year (assuming no principal repayment). If interest rates go up by three quarters of a percent, you will now be paying 8.25 percent and your annual cost of borrowing will be $8,250. You are worse off when interest rates rise and better off when they fall.

It is difficult to predict interest rates and market conditions and this can make it difficult to predict cash flows. You may end up with a much higher interest expense than planned.

Businesses that are exposed to significant interest rate risk use a variety of means to hedge that risk, including interest rate swaps, options, and forward contracts, all of which are beyond the scope of this book. Speak to your accountant for more information.

If you are exposed to only moderate interest rate risk, make sure that it is survivable. When projecting cash flows, look at "what if" scenarios. What would happen if interest rates went up by 1 percent? 5 percent? If your cash flows are tight in the start-up period and you cannot survive interest rate risk, make sure that all your debt financing is fixed rate.

Foreign Exchange Risk

This type of risk happens when the money coming into your business is denominated in a different currency than the money going out. For example, if you sell most of your product in yen and you pay most of your expenses in US dollars, you are better off when the US dollar rises against the yen and worse off when it falls. If both your revenues and your expenses are in the same currency, there is no risk because, if your revenues go up, your expenses go up and vice versa. This type of risk can squeeze your profit margins in much the same way a fixed price agreement or interest rate risk can.

It is impractical and unwise to simply avoid foreign sales because of the potential risk. There are many sophisticated hedging strategies that you can employ to minimize or get rid of the risk completely. To see an example of a currency option contract, please refer to the second book in the *Numbers 101 for Small Business* series, *Financial Management 101.*

Economic Dependence

If your business relies on one or only a few customers for all of its revenues, then your business is economically dependent. If losing one of your major customers would put your business in jeopardy, you are at risk of insolvency.

Economic dependence can be a difficult risk to eliminate, especially in the start-up years, when you may only start out with a few customers. Make sure that you continually seek new customers and new markets to make sure that you're not putting all your eggs in one basket.

Chapter Summary

➡ Along with the rewards in your business come many risks that you need to get a handle on and minimize.

➡ Securing loans with personal or business assets or with personal guarantees can get you a lower interest rate but expose you and your business to the risk of losing the assets.

➡ Fixed price agreements can lock you into an unfavorable arrangement unless properly structured.

➡ Interest rate and foreign exchange risk can squeeze profits and cause insolvency unless hedged.

Chapter
10

Home Sweet Home

Should you operate your business out of your home of should you rent or buy space? We look at the variables to consider.

Introduction

It's 8:30 in the morning. You're still in your pajamas, having just ushered your kids and spouse out the door to school and work, respectively. You take a moment to stack the breakfast dishes neatly in the dishwasher, then pour yourself another cup of coffee. Fifteen minutes later, you're showered and dressed in comfortable clothes and are checking your e-mails on your computer in the office set up in your spare bedroom. At 10:30 a.m., you stretch and grab another coffee, taking enough time to throw a load of laundry in the washer. Your 3:00 p.m. break allows you to put dinner in the oven and spend a little time with your children as they arrive home from school. It is the idyllic home office situation. Unfortunately, the reality is frequently very different than the dream.

Many entrepreneurs choose to start their small businesses out of their homes to begin with. This definitely saves money and can

CASE STUDY

Although EarthPower would have sales offices in Brussels and Atlanta, the management end would be run out of Craig's basement office until the company was able to find a suitable office space. Marnie was excited that her husband would be so close to home but Craig wondered if the arrangement would be feasible.

He got his answer soon enough. Unlike the home-based businesses of several of his college friends, Craig's home office arrangement worked very well. His partner spent much of his time in Brussels setting up the new sales office so Craig was left to build up the operational side. It would be at least six months before their projected cash flows would allow them to hire a full-time administrative assistant, so Craig was trying to split his time between telephone calls, bookkeeping, marketing, and on-shore sales.

The Tuesday before Thanksgiving, Craig "hit the wall." He was on a conference call with Brussels on the telephone. He was also speaking intermittently on his cell phone with a potential supplier from Charleston. The desk in front of him was piled high with typical business paperwork: invoices, billings, bank statements, gas receipts, and other assorted detritus. Craig ended his telephone conversation with Brussels and focused on his cell phone. He paced the floor as he spoke with the supplier, intentionally turning his back on the mountain of paperwork.

Then it happened. The business phone rang again. Craig felt his blood pressure rise. He was completely overwhelmed. It was then that Marnie appeared at the bottom of the basement stairs, a baby monitor in her

reduce the risk that would exist if they lock into a lease agreement on office space.

There are many considerations to keep in mind when you are deciding whether it makes sense to operate your business from your home or to lease office space. Some of these considerations are financial, while others relate to the effect of working from home on your personal life.

Does It Really Save Me Money?

When deciding whether or not to work from a home office, financial considerations come to the forefront, especially when you are first starting out. You are already paying all the expenses on your home whether or not you have your business there: the mortgage or rent, utilities, property taxes, maintenance, and a host of other costs. It may at first seem like it would be "free" to have your business operate out of your house. There are a few issues with that supposition, however:

- **Your house insurance may not cover a business.** You may have to get a separate insurance policy to cover the loss of business assets in your home or to cover the interruption in your business if something catastrophic happens, like a burst water pipe. This is an added expense that you will have to factor into your decision.

- **The zoning of your neighborhood may be residential only and may not allow a business to operate.** Check with your local zoning office to find out whether it's even possible for you to operate out of your home. Zoning officials will most likely ask you things like how many customers do you expect to have in the house and what type and how much parking you have available. You may have to pay extra fees or property taxes to the municipality in order to be able to operate a business.

- **You will be subsidizing the operating costs of your business.** This will definitely help to save money in the start-up phase of your business, but it may allow you to operate a business that wouldn't survive without that subsidy. Previously in this book, we discussed the fact that all businesses that are built on successful and sustainable models can pay all of their expenses and provide a return to the owners. Your business, if it is to be successful and have value that can be transferred to a buyer, must eventually be able to operate from leased or purchased premises. Not paying any premises expenses may lull you into thinking that your business is successful when it is truly not. If you work from home in the start-up period but plan on moving to a separate location in the future, make sure that you have tracked that cost in your cash flow projections.

How Will It Affect My Personal Life?

Once you have examined the financial considerations of whether to operate from your home, there are some practical issues that should be looked at as well.

The neighbors

Your neighbors might not be as enthused as you are about your new enterprise, especially if it results in increased traffic volumes on what would otherwise be a quiet residential street. If you run a business where you work from home but see your customers at their homes or places of business, you will not run into this issue.

If, on the other hand, you plan on having your customers come to your home office (and assuming your neighborhood is suitably zoned), it makes sense to discuss it with your neighbors first. You are not asking their permission; you are simply informing them as a courtesy and encouraging them to bring any concerns to your attention immediately instead of going to the municipality to complain. Who knows, your neighbors might end up being some of your best customers!

The on-call syndrome

When I first started my accounting and consulting practice from an office in my home, I thought I had set it up perfectly. All client meetings were by appointment only, so that I would always know when a client was coming. This gave me time to make sure my home office was tidy and that I was professionally dressed. My office hours were from 9 a.m. to 5 p.m. so that clients could call and reach me during those times.

That setup worked well for about the first week. But thereafter, clients started dropping in: "Well, I was just in the neighborhood and I knew you'd be here." Not only did this happen during the day, but also in the evenings and on weekends. I began to feel trapped in my own home, never being able to spend a lazy Saturday morning in my pajamas reading the newspaper or in my "grubby clothes" gardening in the yard for fear that there would be a knock at the door. Clients also called at all times of the day

CASE STUDY
continued

hand. Craig knew that he couldn't handle family issues at the moment on top of everything else. He motioned to the cell phone, indicating he was busy but Marnie simply sat at the desk and answered the telephone.

"EarthPower Systems. This is Marnie." As she spoke to the caller, she extricated a notepad from the pile, picked up a pen from the floor and took notes. Craig could only stare as she ended the call, handed him the message slip, and picked up the leaning pile of papers on the desk, along with a long-neglected and dusty box of file folders, and disappeared back upstairs.

Marnie helped EarthPower organize its books and records and also answered the telephones when Craig's life got hectic (and when the baby was asleep). She would not have been able to do that if the business did not operate from their basement. The flexibility of the location allowed EarthPower resources that they would otherwise not have had.

and night. I began to turn the ringer on the business telephone off at 5 p.m. so that I didn't have to ignore it.

Even if you set parameters on your availability, there is a probability that your customers will not always honor those limits. If you are the type of person who wants to create a distinct separation between your home life and your working life, you may not want to have a home office. If you do choose to have customers come to your home, here are some tips to make it easier on you and your family:

- Have a separate entrance for your home office. That way, if you do have unexpected customers, you do not have to traipse them through the kids' playroom and the kitchen stacked high with dirty dishes.

- Communicate your meeting and telephone policies with all of your customers. Make sure they understand what is acceptable and not acceptable. Put a sign on the office entrance door with your hours of operation and information on making appointments.

- Be firm but professional with customers who show up unexpectedly. Explain to them (once again) that they will need to make an appointment so that you can be more prepared for them.

- Have a separate telephone and fax line for the business from your home line. Turn off the ringer on the office telephone when outside of office hours. Record a telephone message reiterating your office hours and that you will be pleased to return the call during those hours.

The convenience

So far, we've looked mainly at the down side of working from home. For many entrepreneurs, however, this arrangement works well and allows them the flexibility to balance work and family responsibilities.

Having a home office will definitely save you commuting time, time that can be spent more effectively on managing and growing your business. It also can allow you to be home when your children get home from school, thereby saving on child care fees, or when service people have to come to your home to make repairs. If you can discipline yourself well enough, having a home office will let you structure your day more efficiently around family needs.

Willpower

When you work at an office outside the home, you have a clear divide between work time and home time. You know that when you are in the office, you are there for one reason: to work. This is not so clear when you have a home office, and if your willpower and ability to monitor yourself is weak, you may find yourself doing more lounging than working. Taking "just fifteen minutes" to catch "The Price Is Right" or to take a quick swim in the pool can often turn into the majority of the day.

To corral this problem, take some time first thing every morning to plan your day. Make a list of everything that you need and want to accomplish that day and prioritize them. Block time off in your calendar not only for your scheduled appointments but also to work on your tasks. For example, if you want to get a quote out to a customer by 5 p.m., block off an hour (if that's how long you think it will take) to work on the quote. This will help you make sure that you are not over-committing yourself and setting yourself up for failure. It also helps you to structure your day so that you are being as productive as you are able.

Chapter Summary

➡ There are many financial considerations involved in deciding whether working from a home office makes sense, including zoning, parking, and insurance.

➡ A home office can afford you more flexibility in balancing your home and work lives.

➡ It is important to be clear with your customers as to your available hours for telephone or face-to-face meetings.

➡ Working from home will require you to structure your time to ensure that you are being as productive as possible.

Chapter
11

Choosing Your External Team

No business survives for the long term without a great team of advisers: lawyers, accountants, financial planners, and a board of directors. We look at how to choose your advisory team and what questions you should be asking them.

Introduction

As you begin your new business, there will be no bigger factor in your success or failure than your choice of your business's advisers. Your lawyer, accountant, financial adviser, and board of directors will fill in the gaps in your own skills and will be valuable sources of information as you grow.

As a new entrepreneur, you may decide that this is an area in which you want to save money, being the scarce resource that it is. I highly recommend, however, that you invest in good external advisers. A few hundred dollars now can save you a few thousand (or more!) later.

CASE STUDY

"A board of directors? Are you serious?" Craig's partner, Gordon, looked at Vivian skeptically. "We're not Microsoft, you know."

Vivian said, "An independent board of directors is important for even the smallest of companies. A board can review your operations with a fresh set of eyes and perhaps find looming roadblocks or lucrative opportunities that you and Craig have missed because you both are so involved in the day-to-day operations of the company."

"Well," Craig said, "I guess it doesn't hurt to have a second opinion sometimes. I know we both feel like we're in over our heads at times."

"That's the purpose of a board of directors," said Vivian. "To help guide the company."

Craig turned to his partner. "What about John Wendsley?"

"The founder of Wendsley Motors?" Gordon asked. "He's retired now."

"I know. That's why he'd be perfect. He spent his lifetime building his business. Now he's retired and working on some volunteer projects. I think he might like to help out a new company," Craig said. "And he has an incredible amount of experience in building a business."

Vivian said, "That's a good start. Now let's make up a list of your potential board members and plan how we're going to present the opportunity to them."

Chosen well, your external advisers can help you with the following:

- Provide guidance on your business's direction and growth strategy
- Connect you with lenders and investors to which you would otherwise have no knowledge of or way of approaching
- Find potential acquisition targets to fuel your business growth
- Troubleshoot roadblocks and other obstacles in which you lack experience

Finding the perfect fit in an adviser can seem like a daunting task when you're first starting out. You may find it difficult to know how to assess qualifications and experience. Let's have a look at your main group of advisers and what you will need to take into consideration when searching for the right ones.

Your Lawyer

You will need a lawyer to advise your small business on many issues, including the following:

- Incorporation
- Labor laws
- Contracts (with customers, suppliers, and employees)
- Mergers and acquisitions
- Estate planning matters
- Exit strategies
- Personal wills and powers of attorney

You will most likely start with a general practitioner who can handle most of the day-to-day legal work your business needs, and then hire specialists for everything else. A good general practitioner will have experience in many different areas and will know when to bring in a specialist. He or she will also be able to recommend one to you. Make sure that your prospective lawyer has experience with small businesses and doesn't mostly deal only with personal or family legal matters.

In the United States, each state has its own bar association that regulates the lawyers of that state. In Canada, the Canadian Bar Association regulates lawyers. These associations can help you find a lawyer in your community that specializes in small businesses.

Meet with him or her and assess how well the two of you communicate. Find out about his or her billing practices and whether a retainer (an amount of money paid in advance of work being undertaken) is required. Make sure to tell the lawyer about your personal situation as well so that he or she can see the whole picture and can make recommendations on wills, estates, and exit strategy planning.

Your Accountant

One of the areas that many entrepreneurs are weak in is finance and accounting. Their backgrounds have generally not allowed them sufficient exposure to this critical foundation wall of any business.

The right accountant can help you in several areas:

- Selecting and setting up your record keeping system
- Developing your monthly management operating plan
- Defining your key success factors
- Preparing cash flow projections
- Tax planning
- Exit strategy planning
- Mergers and acquisitions
- Human resource interviewing and screening
- Growth strategies
- Estate planning

As you can see, accountants are far more than "bean counters." But how do you know when you have found the right one? Here are some strategies to help you select an accountant:

1. **Talk to your business associates.** They can be a great source of referral for an accountant. Ask your associates not only questions about the competency of the accountant but also about their relationship. Ultimately, you will need an accountant that speaks the language of the small-business owner, not "accountant talk."

2. **Review the websites of the professional accounting bodies in your jurisdiction.** Each professional organization will have regulated training and experience requirements that individuals will have to perform before receiving their

professional designation. Remember, too, that the word "accountant" is not regulated the way the word "lawyer" is. Anyone can call himself or herself an accountant and prepare financial statements and tax returns. It's important to delve into the qualifications of the person you're about to hire.

In the United States, professional accountants are called Certified Public Accountants (CPAs) and are regulated by the American Institute of Certified Public Accountants (www.aicpa.org). In Canada, chartered accountants are regulated by the Canadian Institute of Chartered Accountants (www.cica.ca), certified management accountants are regulated by the Society of Management Accountants of Canada (www.cma-canada.org), and certified general accountants are regulated by the Certified General Accountants Association of Canada (www.cga-canada.org). At the time of printing of this book, the associations regulating the chartered accountants and certified management accountants are proposing a merger of the two bodies.

Each of these designations carries with them differing levels of training and experience requirements. The websites can also direct you to local members.

3. **Meet with the prospective accountant.** This initial "get to know you" meeting should come at no charge to you, but ask if that's the case ahead of time. In the years to come, you will have to be able to communicate well with the accountant, understand what he or she is telling you, and trust the information being imparted to you. Never underestimate your feelings about the accountant at this first meeting. You should feel that the two of you "click." At this meeting you should also discuss the accountant's areas of expertise, number of clients (you don't want to be the first client but you also don't want to be a tiny fish in an ocean), and billing policies and rates.

4. **Ask for references.** The accountant should be able to give you the names of several small-business clients similar to yourself that you can call and ask questions about their relationship with the accountant. Note that because of confidentiality issues, the accountant will first have to get permission from the clients to use them as references.

As with all of your advisers, don't rush into hiring an accountant. Take your time and it will certainly pay off in the long run.

Your Financial Adviser

In most jurisdictions, the term "financial planner" is as unregulated as "accountant." Anyone can call himself or herself a financial planner. Of all your advisers, your choice of financial planner can have the greatest impact on your personal and business wealth.

What do financial planners actually do for you? It depends on whom you choose, but most financial planners can do the following:

- Draw up an investment plan for your retirement
- Recommend the mix of investments that your portfolio should have
- Recommend specific investments and even be able to purchase them on your behalf
- Help you determine your insurance needs
- Recommend other financial products, such as mortgages and tax-deferred shelters

It is critical to find an accountant and financial planner who work well together. Their areas of expertise will overlap and it's important that they're on the same page. All tax strategies recommended by your financial planner should be agreed to by your accountant and any investment strategy organized by your accountant should be vetted by your financial planner. Once you find an accountant that you trust, he or she is likely a good source of recommendation for a financial planner.

It's also important to find an independent planner. This means that the planner is not connected to nor gets paid by investment companies. You want to make sure that the planner is working in your best interest, not the best interest of lining his or her pocket. Financial planners get paid in different ways depending upon how they operate and the size and type of portfolio you have:

- **Commissions.** Some planners receive commissions from the mutual fund and insurance companies whose products are sold through them. For example, with this type of arrangement, if you were to purchase $10,000 worth of mutual fund units through your planner, the fund company would pay the planner a commission. You would not have to pay anything. Although this seems like a good idea for you, it may not be in the long run if the planner is simply recommending the product on which he or she receives the most commission. In this type of fee arrangement, it's important to find a planner who deals with multiple companies and can "shop your business around" for you, much like an insurance broker.

- **Hourly fee.** Some planners work much like accountants and lawyers and will charge you by the hour to work on your financial plan.
- **Asset-based fees.** Some planners will charge a fee based on a percentage (usually half to 1 percent) of the assets in your portfolio to manage that portfolio. This generally only happens if you have a large portfolio.

Once you have decided upon your financial planner, make sure you meet with him or her at least annually to review the financial plan. Your planner can explain the growth in your assets in the previous year based on what has happened in world markets, and can review the plan to make sure that you are still on track for the upcoming year.

Your Board of Directors

When you think of the phrase "board of directors," mammoth companies like Microsoft and General Motors probably spring immediately to mind. Every corporation, however, regardless of size, is required to maintain a board of directors. Even if your business is not incorporated, it is advisable to have at least an informal board.

The board of directors is a slate of advisers chosen by the shareholders of the company to advise and guide management. Especially in larger companies, the board is mostly made up of external members, that is to say those that do not also work in the company. They may be business owners or managers themselves. The incorporation documents of the company outline the board's duties and responsibilities, including which issues must be voted on by the board.

In a small company, getting external board members may be difficult, but it is even more critical than for a larger organization. Experienced board members bring knowledge and advisory skills to the table that you may lack. If nothing else, they bring new ideas and opinions.

So why would someone want to sit on your board of directors? Certainly not for the cold hard cash. Fewer than 50 percent of companies pay their boards, and those that do, pay a pittance. Most directors sit on boards for the pleasure of helping guide a fledgling company, the same reason that you're an entrepreneur.

To find your directors, start by making a list of those business owners and managers in your community whom you trust and respect and who are not afraid of voicing their opinions. For this reason, you will not want to include friends and family as they may be too concerned with hurting your feelings to tell you that you are driving the company into the ground. Speak with those on your list about your need for guidance in your new venture. Even those who choose to decline the offer of being on the board may extend other offers, such as being available to offer advice or hooking you up with investors and lenders.

One last word about directors. The directors of a corporation are legally liable for everything the company does, which may be one reason that those on your list shy away from the responsibility. There is a type of insurance product that provides some protection to the directors and your directors may insist that you take out such a policy, so make sure that you calculate the premiums into your cash flows.

Chapter Summary

➡ Your team of external advisers is made up of your lawyer, accountant, financial planner, and board of directors.

➡ The main role of your external advisers is to fill in the gaps in your knowledge and experience so that your business can avoid pitfalls and flourish.

➡ One of the best ways to find your accountant and lawyer is through speaking with other small-business owners in your community.

➡ Your board of directors will be charged with the task of guiding the company in all major decisions and should be chosen carefully.

Chapter 12

Assessing the Competition

In this chapter, we turn to competitive analysis. What are the other companies in your industry doing well? Doing badly?

Introduction

What first comes to mind when you hear the phrase "competitive intelligence"? Slinking around in the bushes with a pair of binoculars and a notepad, eating stale donuts and drinking cold coffee, hoping for a single glimpse of something illusive and perhaps illicit? Or a James Bond-type character dressed to kill and sipping a martini (shaken not stirred), snapping pictures of forbidden foreign documents with a cufflink camera? Well, unfortunately, the real world of competitive intelligence isn't nearly as glamorous as all that.

Competitive intelligence is something that every smart entrepreneur does on a continual basis. It is simply the process of uncovering, analyzing, and presenting publicly available information on your business's competitors in order to maintain a competitive advantage in the marketplace.

CASE STUDY

"Tell me about Green Source Inc.," Vivian said the next day when she and the two partners met again.

Craig shrugged his shoulders. "I don't know. They're a new company based out of Atlanta. They seem to be selling the same types of products we are, but I haven't been paying much attention to them."

Gordon chimed in. "If we pay too much attention to them, it'll look like we're scared."

Vivian said, "On the contrary. Paying close attention to your competition is what smart companies do. You can learn lots from finding out how they're approaching potential customers, what their marketing message is, and what their pricing looks like."

"But we don't want to copy them," Craig protested. "We want to be the market leader."

"How will you know if you're leading if you don't know who's following you and where they are in the race?" asked Vivian. "You have to understand your competition inside and out and be able to articulate what your market niche is compared to theirs and how your products and services are superior."

"They're running a seminar on wind power over at the Arena next Wednesday. Do you think we should go?" asked Craig.

Vivian said, "I think that's a good start. Then, let's make a list of all the things we want to know about the competition and we'll list ideas on how to obtain that information."

In Chapter 5, we looked at preparing the business plan, in which you outline your business's niche and position in the industry. Competitive intelligence is the tool to research the background information. As the owner and manager (and chief bottle washer) of your business, the competitive intelligence job will most likely fall to you. It becomes an integral part of your ongoing analysis of your own operations as well as the entire operating environment. Competitive intelligence will tell you what products or services you should be offering, how you can present them to existing and potential customers, and how to improve your position in your industry relative to your competitors.

Let's have a look at the steps to take in order to analyze your competition.

Identify the Competition

Do you know who your competitors are? Start by opening the telephone book and scanning the Yellow Pages or the business directory. If you are a bookstore, your most direct competitors are the other bookstores in your local area. They will all be listed alongside your business in the telephone book.

Your list of competitors stretches beyond the list of direct competitors, however. It includes those providers who can deliver the same product or service as you do through another distribution channel, such as over the internet or through trade shows. Staying with the bookstore example, it would mean that you are also in competition with amazon.com, for example.

Your competitors also include businesses that can deliver a different product or service that accomplishes the same goal. This means that your bookstore must not only compete for book business but for entertainment business. You are competing with movie theaters, dance clubs, and cable networks.

Having a solid understanding of the competitors in your market will help you to better understand your own business and its place in the competitive environment.

What Do They Do Right and Wrong?

Once you have determined who the competition is, it's time to evaluate what is working for them and against them.

Start a file on each of your major competitors. Gather as much of their marketing, promotional, and sales material as possible. Print off pages from their website. Cut out display ads from the newspaper and magazines. Listen to their speeches and presentations.

Review all of the printed material. What kind of image is this competitor portraying? If you were a potential customer, what would attract you to this business? What type of customer are they trying to appeal to? Is it exactly the same market as you are targeting or are they appealing to a customer base you haven't before contemplated? Do they have products or services that you don't offer your customers? Do they use better technology and equipment than you do?

Where is this business weak? Is their location difficult to find? Are they understaffed? Overpriced?

Call the business as if you were a potential customer. How are you greeted when you call? Are they helpful and friendly or indifferent?

As you go through this process with each of your major competitors, do not discount your feelings about the business. Customers will make their buy/don't buy decision based on their immediate perceptions of a business, so keep in mind what perceptions you are forming from your analysis.

How Are They Positioned to Take Advantage of Opportunities?

Opportunities occur outside the control of a business. Each business will be differently positioned to be able to take advantage of these opportunities. For example, if one of your new competitors is highly leveraged (that is to say, has bought a lot of equipment and tools on credit), they may not be able to buy an existing business if it suddenly comes up for sale. How are your competitors positioned to be able to take advantage of new technology in your industry? Will they be able to retool in time to capture new customer bases or are they already sinking under their management structure?

How Vulnerable Are They to Changing Market Conditions?

The other side of being able to take advantage of opportunities is being able to react to external threats. Threats can include things like changing tax laws, legal action, new competitors, and theft — all things that are potential land mines for businesses that are not prepared.

Does the structure of your competitors hinder their ability to respond to threats? For example, if you are in the tire recycling business, how would each of your competitors be able to deal with new regulations restricting the storage of used tires? Would some be out of business?

How Do You Stack Up?

The ultimate goal of collecting all of this competitive information is to be able to use it to your advantage. Compare yourself to your competitors based on your research, and answer these questions:

1. Are there other products or services I should be offering my customers?

2. Should I offer higher quality products or services?

3. Are there other customer groups I should be targeting?

4. How can we improve our customer service to make our customers more loyal?

5. What can we improve in our marketing, promotional, and sales materials to better communicate who we are to our customers?

6. Should we be upgrading our equipment to be able to save us money or produce more efficiently?

7. Should we be accepting more forms of payment to make it easier for our customers to pay us?

8. Can we pursue more free media attention?

9. Are there networking opportunities that we should be pursuing?

10. How can we position ourselves to be better able to capitalize on opportunities and weather threats?

Competitive analysis is an ongoing process of keeping apprised of the ever-changing nature of the market in which you operate. You need to regularly monitor your competitors to see how they evolve and grow. If they're smart, they'll be monitoring you too!

SWOT ANALYSIS

In MBA-speak, the analysis we discussed above is called a SWOT analysis:

Strengths

Weaknesses

Opportunities

Threats

A business's strengths and weaknesses are those qualities internal to the business, those things that are under the business's control. Opportunities and threats come from the external operating environment and are events to which the business must react.

A SWOT analysis helps a business to identify its best and worst qualities and allows the business to have a deeper understanding of how to find opportunities and weather threats.

Competitive Analysis

One way to keep all of your competitive analysis organized is to set up a binder with a section for each of your major competitors. Keep the summary research all on one page for each competitor and file their marketing, promotional, and sales material in behind. You may wish to use or modify Worksheet 2 to do a competitive analysis for your business.

Intelligence Resources

With the advent of the World Wide Web, it is easier than ever to research your competitors. Here are some resources that you can use to assist your research:

- **Web search engines,** such as Google (www.google.com). In a search engine, you simply type in the words that you are looking for and the engine lists all of the web pages that contain those words. You will frequently have to narrow down your search to make sure that you are getting the most relevant results. You may find links to your competitor's website, advertising, and upcoming event listings, and chat rooms where customers are discussing the product or service.

WORKSHEET 2
COMPETITIVE ANALYSIS

Business name:

Address:

Contacts:

Years in business:

Products or services:

Pricing structure

Strengths	Weaknesses
Opportunities	Threats

Other notes:

- **News monitoring or Web clipping services.** Some of these services are free and some are subscription based. News monitoring services scour the Web for news articles containing words that you specify. You can request, for example, that you be notified when there are articles or news stories generated that contain the words "Microsoft Corp."

- **Corporate website.** Many businesses maintain their own websites. Some of these sites are simply an online representation of the business brochure. On some, you can order products or services, ask questions, and drill down into the details of products or services being offered. Your competitors' websites will give you a good idea of how the businesses present themselves and what they perceive to be their strengths. If your competitors don't have websites, you may wish to consider developing one for your business to give you a competitive advantage.

Chapter Summary

➡ Competitive intelligence is the gathering, analyzing, and using of publicly available information about the competitors in your industry.

➡ Research and analysis of your competitors includes gathering all marketing, promotional, and sales material as well as visiting the business and attending speeches and events hosted by the business.

➡ Competitive intelligence is an ongoing process to continually monitor the ever-changing nature of the environment in which you operate.

➡ There are many internet-based tools that you can incorporate into your competitive analysis process.

C h a p t e r

13

Forecasting Profit

A re you going to be able to meet payroll next week? Make the interest and principal payments on your business loans next month? We look at how to forecast and plan cash flows for smooth sailing.

Introduction

In earlier chapters, we discussed how you will forecast your cash flow to ascertain whether your business idea is a good one and also to be able to present information to lenders and investors.

In this chapter, we will talk about continual forecasting, that is, how to make sure that your business is both making a profit and providing positive cash flow to finance growth and expansion. You will need this information to know if you're on track with your plan and also to be able to attract new sources of financing. There are a number of areas to focus on to ensure that your cash management stays an important part of your business.

Keep Your Bookkeeping Up-to-Date

If you're like most small-business owners, this probably isn't the most fun or fulfilling part of your job, but it is definitely one of the most critical. The only way that you will be able to accurately predict your financing needs is by tracking your business's current performance. Keeping accurate records will also tell you which suppliers need to be paid to avoid penalties and interest, and which customers are overdue in their payments. Make sure you set aside some time every day to record the bookkeeping for the prior day.

Always Forecast a Rolling 12 Months

When you first started your business, you prepared a 12-month and 5-year cash flow projection. The 12-month projection should be a living, breathing entity, which you will update on a monthly basis. The term "rolling" 12 months simply means that as one month drops into history, you will project out another one. For example, if it's now February 2005, your 12-month projection will encompass March 2005 to February 2006. In March 2005, the projection will drop March 2005 (as it has already happened) and add in March 2006. With this method, you will always know what lies ahead for the next 12 months. The projection will warn you if you are going to run out of cash at any point in the next year. Then you can prepare by sourcing financing to cover the shortfall rather than be startled by it when your bank balance is zero.

Tighten Up Billing and Collection Policies

Managing your operating funds is critical to every small business and lack of control over these issues sinks a good number of businesses. Take some time to review your billing and credit policies. Are they in line with your competitors? Do you extend credit too freely? Too stingily? How are the receivables being followed up? Is it being done consistently?

If you find that receivables management tends to be one of the last things you hastily do, you may want to consider hiring an accounts receivable clerk to manage the funds coming in. It's critical to make sure that the money comes in as regularly as you have predicted in your cash flow statement. You can have a highly profitable business and still go bankrupt because customers aren't paying you on time. For a more in-depth discussion of accounts receivable policies, please refer to the second book in the *Numbers 101 for Small Business* series, *Financial Management 101*.

Hire Someone to Do It If You Can't

As you will quickly learn in operating your business, you can't do everything, although small-business owners give it their best shot. You will have to continually analyze the consequences of things falling through the cracks. For example, if accounts payable isn't done regularly, you may be incurring significant penalties and interest on late payments or NSF checks. If you have too much work for one person to do, you could be losing customers. If you don't keep up with your forecasting, you may suddenly run out of cash. Know when to hire someone and what you most need done. For a more in-depth discussion of hiring, please refer to Chapter 14.

Keep on Top of Changes in the Operating Environment

In Chapter 12, we discussed assessing your competition, their internal strengths and weaknesses, and how they will be able to react to external opportunities and threats. It's every bit as important for you to continually analyze the environment in which your business operates and assess how you are positioned to take advantage of opportunities and deal with roadblocks.

Formalize this analysis as part of your day. Stay on top of changes in the industry by reading industry publications and networking with other small-business owners, both those in your particular industry and those who operate businesses in the same community as you. Join your local Chamber of Commerce to find out what's happening in the world of small business. Talk to your accountant about pending changes in tax and audit laws.

The more informed you are, the better you will be able to finance the future.

Keep the Work Coming In

You may sometimes feel that you will be fine once you finish the mound of work you have on your plate right now and can rest for a few minutes. One very serious mistake made frequently by small-business owners is to concentrate only on today's work without considering where the work will come from tomorrow. As a small-business owner, you have three heads: one that looks back to the past to learn from history, one that's focused on the here and now and the things that need to be accomplished today, and one that looks to the future, to figure out what work needs to be generated in order to meet your revenue targets.

Always keep an eye on future work. It's only work that gets brought in, done, billed, and collected that will result in cash in your bank account. Make sure that there are no gaps in that stream of cash.

Continually Assess New Sources of Financing

Once you have your initial source of financing in place, you may think that your need for cash has ended, but a wise entrepreneur always has his or her eye on the financial markets. You may need to replace your initial source of financing some day and you will need to know what the new cost of capital will be because it will affect your cash flow projections. You may have a sudden opportunity to purchase another business in your industry and will want to have already done your homework with respect to sources and cost of capital.

Make sure you spend time talking with your accountant and your financial planner about your existing and projected cash needs. They may be able to help you with your future needs.

Chapter Summary

➡ Cash flow projections should be an ongoing and integral part of your management operating plan.

➡ Keeping your historical financial bookkeeping up to date is critical to being able to predict future problems.

➡ Assess the need to hire an employee to help keep you on top of financial recording and planning if you are unable to do it by yourself.

➡ Continually assess new sources of financing in case you need to replace your existing funding or need money for expansion.

Investing in Labor

Without your staff, your business wouldn't exist. But when is it time to hire? Will another employee pay for himself or herself? We look at the issues surrounding getting the most out of your investment in your employees.

Introduction

If you start out like most small businesses, there will be only you in the beginning. You will be the manager, sales director, administration assistant, and office cleaner. As your business grows, you will be constantly assessing whether you will be better off to hire an employee or to simply work harder and reap more of the profits for yourself.

The decision process for hiring labor is much like the process for any other type of capital investment. I use the term "capital investment" because the cost of an employee is not like most other operating expenses you will incur, but is more like an investment. You will spend money to "purchase" the labor, but will receive a greater return on investment over time than the amount originally

CASE STUDY

"We've got to spend more time developing the US market," Craig's partner, Gordon, said.

"I know we do but I'm just snowed under with all of the administrative details. And you're always in Europe." Craig poured a cup of coffee. "Even with Marnie helping out, we're still way too busy."

"I think it's time we hire a full-time office manager," Gordon said.

"But it's too early; we didn't plan to do that until month six," Craig said.

"Just think about the potential sales we're losing because you're stuck doing all the paperwork. Let's rework the cash flows assuming that you'll be able to spend 80 percent of your time talking with potential customers."

Later that afternoon, Craig reviewed the projections. "We could have doubled our sales if I had been able to spend more time with potential customers. Trying to save money really got us behind."

Gordon said, "Well, let's start the process of hiring an office manager now. Then we can get back on track."

invested. For example, if it costs you $30,000 a year to hire an employee, and he or she is able to bill out $47,000 of his or her time to your customers, you are receiving a 57 percent return on your investment.

The decision is rarely as cut and dried as this, however. Frequently, employees need to be hired in advance of the expected increase in revenues and the question then becomes, when is the right time? You don't want to incur unnecessary expenses on the one hand, but you also don't want to work yourself into an early grave on the other. This chapter looks at some of the considerations to ponder when deciding whether or not and when to hire.

The Cost of an Employee

When assessing how much it will cost you to hire an employee, it's important to take into consideration all of the costs involved, including some of the following.

Salary

This is the most obvious one. It is the amount that you quote to the employee when hiring. Wages can be either in the form of a fixed annual salary (e.g., $25,000 per year), or an hourly rate (e.g., $7.50 per hour). If you plan on paying hourly, you will need to estimate how many hours the employee will work in a standard year. A typical work year is around 1,950 hours, taking into account holidays and vacation time.

The quoted salary or hourly rate will not end up being the amount the employee pockets however. Depending upon the jurisdiction in which you operate, you may be required to deduct income taxes, pension contributions, unemployment premiums, or health care premiums. This does not matter to your calculations, however, as you will be spending the entire amount, even though you will be giving some to the government.

Employer taxes

In some jurisdictions, you will be required to pay additional amounts to the government for pension, unemployment, and health care premiums on top of what you have withheld from your employee. These amounts are usually based on the dollar amount of your total payroll. Ask your accountant for the amounts and rates and be sure to take these additional costs into account.

Office space

When you hire an employee, you will need to have a space for him or her to work in as well as additional office supplies and equipment, like a desk, workbench, telephone, and computer. List out all of these additional items that you will need for a new employee and estimate the cost.

You may instead decide to have your employee work from his or her own home. This is called telecommuting. This is one way that you can lower your labor costs and still get the help you need.

Fringe benefits

In order to attract quality employees, small-business owners make their businesses more attractive to potential employees by offering benefits other than salary. These benefits might include health care, life insurance, gym memberships, baseball or hockey tickets, and a host of other incentives. If you will be offering any of these to your employees, calculate and factor in the cost of these additional benefits.

Calculating the Benefit

Now that you know how much it will cost to hire an employee, what will be the benefit to your business? This will partly be determined by what role the employee will play in the business. It is easier to calculate the benefit if the employee will be directly connected to the production of the product or service. For example, if you are hiring another hairstylist, you can compare the cost of the new stylist to the projected revenues that he or she will bring in. It's a much more difficult task to calculate the benefit of hiring a receptionist, who is critical to the successful operation of your business but doesn't directly bring revenues in the door.

Let's have a look at each of these types of employees.

Direct labor

This type of employee will actually do some of the work that the business does. He or she will be building widgets or providing services to your customers. To calculate the benefit of hiring direct labor, estimate how many units the employee can make of the product or how many hours he or she can bill out.

Here's an example.

Roland runs a computer consulting business. He is frequently out on service calls to residential customers who need repairs to their computers or training on new software. Roland is working 60 hours a week and his booking lag is growing. He frequently can't get out to a customer's home within a week of the call and he is losing business because of it.

He has decided to look into hiring another technician in order to be able to handle more service calls. The going rate is $39,450 for a technician, which includes all peripheral expenses. Roland is certain that he can keep the new technician busy full time, both from the current customer base and the new customers that will be pursued when Roland once again has time for marketing. Roland will charge the new tech out at the same rate he charges himself out: $35 per hour. Roland estimates that of the 1,950 hours available in a year, he can bill the technician out for 90 percent of them, or 1,755 hours. The estimated revenue from hiring the new technician will therefore be:

1,755 hours X $35 per hour = $61,425

Roland would therefore make a 56 percent return on his investment in a new technician and he would be farther ahead to hire one than to keep going on as before. Roland can also calculate how many hours he will have to bill the technician out at to break even on his investment:

Break even = $39,450/$35 per hour = 1,127 hours

Therefore, Roland would only have to bill the new technician out for 58 percent of the available hours before he would be worse off.

Indirect labor

This type of employee isn't directly responsible for generating revenues in the business, but is critical to its success. These types of positions might include receptionists, bookkeepers, marketing directors, or delivery people. It's more difficult to quantify the contribution of these employees. Let's look at an example to see how we might do it.

Zoe runs an editing service for small businesses. So far, she's been the sole employee and has performed all of the functions of the business by herself. She has started to notice that she can't keep up with the telephone calls from customers and potential customers and that she is losing business because of it. She estimates that she currently spends 50 percent of her time in actual billable work (at $55 per hour), 40 percent of her time on reception and administration duties, and the other 10 percent of her time on management. Zoe wants to look into the possibility of hiring an office manager to answer telephones and perform most of the administrative duties that Zoe is currently doing. How can we estimate the value of a new employee?

We can look at it from the perspective of what Zoe will gain in productivity. She will be gaining back 40 percent of her time, which she can theoretically bill out to customers. So:

(1,950 hours per year X 40%) X $55 billing rate = $42,900

Therefore, if the cost of an administrative assistant is less than $42,900, Zoe is better off by hiring one than to keep going alone. Zoe will also benefit by retaining more customers and building her customer base, so that, in time, she will be positioned to hire another editor (direct labor).

Your Billing Multiplier

Your billing multiplier is another method of determining when the time is right to hire direct labor. It is calculated by dividing your business's revenues by your direct labor cost. For example, if your revenues are $150,000 and your direct labor cost is $51,250, the billing multiplier is 2.93. The higher the multiple, the more revenues you are earning per unit of labor.

You can compare your multiple to the industry average or to your own multiple over time. To find out what the average is for your industry, start by speaking with your industry association to see if they maintain such statistics. Your accountant may also be able to tell you what's usual. You can track your own multiple over time and, once you have some financial history in your business, you'll be able to tell at what point the multiple tells you that it's time to hire again.

Five Signs It's Time to Hire

Here are five indicators that you may be in a good position to hire someone:

1. **The backlog of work is growing.** If you are noticing that customers must endure longer than average wait times, it may be time to bring someone new on board before customer service levels decline.

2. **Your billing multiplier is rising.** See the above detailed discussion of the billing multiplier.

3. **Your productivity level and that of your existing employees is dropping.** This may be due to "burnout" from trying to work too hard for too long a period of time.

4. **You are well capitalized for growth.** The worst thing that could happen is for you to attract new business with the added employee and not be able to fund the growth.

5. **The pay for overtime is increasing.** If you're finding that you are regularly paying existing staff for working overtime, it's an indication that you may need a new employee. Employees who work chronic overtime are less productive and more prone to burning out.

Chapter Summary

➡ Spending on labor is more like an investment in capital than an operating expense, as you will expect to receive a return on that investment.

➡ When calculating the cost of an employee, make sure to take into consideration all of the peripheral expenses: payroll taxes, fringe benefits, and additional office space and supplies.

➡ Calculating the benefit of hiring a direct labor employee is easier than with an indirect labor employee, but both calculations are important.

➡ If your billing multiplier is high compared to your industry average or to your historical multiplier, it may indicate the need to hire an employee.

Investing in Equipment

Most businesses require equipment to operate, be it computers or rototillers or printing presses. This chapter reviews the balancing of the costs versus the benefits of buying equipment.

Introduction

In most small businesses, the purchase or lease of equipment will be the largest expenditure in the cash flows. As a small-business owner, you will continually be assessing whether to repair or replace old equipment or invest in new equipment. You will be balancing your limited resources (your existing equipment) against your even more limited resource (cash). In the world of financial management, this is called capital budgeting. The term is not important but the concept is. Once you have decided what products and services your business will offer, your job is to ensure that the business does that in the most cost-effective manner, making the most efficient use of equipment.

Equipment encompasses many varied things in a small business. It includes the machinery that your business needs to produce its products, such as metal stamping equipment, injection molds, or table saws. It also includes peripheral equipment, that is, equipment not directly used in the production of goods but important none the less (e.g., computers, cellular telephones, vehicles, and software).

Let's have a look at how we might approach the decision-making process.

To Buy or Not to Buy

The main purpose of any investment is to create value for the investor. Why else would he or she spend the money in the first place?

Let's look at the example of a car. Suppose you're at an estate auction one day and you find a beat-up, paint-chipped 1970 Ford Mustang that, despite its less-than-ideal appearance, runs well. You buy it for $5,000. Your spouse, of course, thinks that you have absolutely lost your mind, but something tells you there is value in the car. You have a friend who does body work and you pay her $3,000 to work on the body and repaint the car. You spend another $200 vacuuming and shampooing the interior and having the car waxed. In total, you have spent $8,200 on the car. You place an ad in the local paper under "Collectible Cars" and you sell the car the next week for $11,000. You have basically been the manager or general contractor of this project and have brought together raw materials (the car) and labor and supplies to create an additional value of $2,800 ($11,000 - $8,200). You are able to pocket the $2,800 and you walk away happy.

The capital budgeting decision tries to identify *before* the investment is made whether there is positive value in a project. When we look at the decision whether or not to purchase equipment, we want to make sure that the purchase will add net value (and net positive cash flows) to the business. In our car example, if we had accurately projected the costs and the revenue from selling the car, we would have calculated the $2,800 in net value. It was easy in that situation as the expenses and revenue happened quite close together in time. With equipment budgeting decisions, the expenses and revenues happen over a longer period of time, so we are comparing today's dollars with future dollars. As we have seen in previous chapters, a dollar in the future is worth less than a dollar today, so we need to look at the discounted cash flows to be able to compare all of the inflows and outflows of cash in the same time frame.

The challenge that we face in capital budgeting is that we can only estimate the future revenue stream (cash inflows). If we estimate incorrectly, we may undertake to purchase equipment that ends up costing us more in the long run than the positive benefits it generates. On the other hand, the equipment that we purchase will most likely be financed, either through bank loans or leases. The expense side of the decision is fixed and, whether or not the new equipment generates the expected revenue levels, bank loans and the lease must be repaid. Therefore, adding leveraged fixed assets to your business involves risk. Careful and accurate estimating and decision analysis can help to soften that risk.

Let's have a look at some of the factors to consider when planning for your equipment purchase.

Erosion

In some business situations, purchasing new equipment allows you to offer new products and services to new groups of customers. This will have a direct positive effect on your revenue stream. On the other hand, where your existing customers will buy the new products and services instead of the old ones, your new equipment will eat into or erode your existing revenue streams. This erosion must be taken into account when estimating your new purchase.

Financing

Especially in the start-up phase of business, your equipment purchases will most likely be financed through a bank loan or through capital leases. Although undertaking these purchases will result in an increase in assets, it will also result in an increase in debt load. This will affect many of your financial statement ratios, including current ratio (current assets/current liabilities) and debt to equity (debt/equity). (For a more in-depth discussion of ratio analysis, please refer to the second book in the *Numbers 101 for Small Business* series, *Financial Management 101*.)

It's important to analyze the entire impact of the purchase. Will you be offside on your bank loan if you increase your debt load? How involved are the other investors in your business supposed to be in the decision? Do you need consensus? What kind of rate can you borrow at to buy this equipment? Frequently, lease rates are difficult to ascertain, so you may need to speak with your accountant about your pending asset purchase to ensure that you are getting the best possible lending rate.

Risk

When assessing the discounted cash flows, the theoretical rule is that you would proceed with any project that has positive discounted cash flows (that is to say, you'll be creating value with those projects). However, in real life, you only have so much cash so it would be impossible to invest in all of the equipment that would make you more money. You have to choose among various projects to find not only the greatest return, but also the least risk.

For example, let's say you own a small bookbinding company with three employees. You are looking to increase your revenues through the purchase of printing equipment. You have $10,000 in available financing. You have found two projects that you feel would help to grow your business, but they are mutually exclusive as each would require a $10,000 investment.

The first option is to purchase another press similar to the one you currently run except that it will be able to print 50 percent faster. This will allow you to run the same types of jobs as you have in the past but you will be able to take on larger orders and larger customers because of the increase in capacity.

The second option is to purchase an on-demand print machine that can produce single copies of books. This is an emerging technology and would allow customers to produce small runs of their self-published books and thereby make publishing a more affordable activity for these types of authors. There are only a few dozen of these "self-serve" type machines in the country and you would be on the leading edge of the technology.

If the expected revenue and cost profiles from both of these investments are exactly the same, you would most likely choose the first one if your main goal was risk reduction. You are comfortable with the technology you currently have and an increase to your capacity would almost certainly increase the bottom line. On the other hand, the new technology used in the second option is unproven and therefore your revenue increase estimates will be softer. The risk of loss from the new product is higher.

However, if your main goal is to be a market leader, you will most likely choose the second option: higher risk but with a greater chance of capturing market share and becoming a leader in the new technology. Once the financial pros and cons have been weighed, the risk and other non-financial facets of the proposals (such as your goals as an entrepreneur) must be considered.

Chapter Summary

➡ As a small-business owner, you will be continually deciding whether to repair existing equipment or buy new.

➡ Discounted cash flows is the method used most frequently to assist with the decision about whether investing in new equipment will pay off.

➡ A small business's cash resources are scarce, so it is impossible to choose all equipment investments that produce positive discounted cash flow.

➡ There are many peripheral considerations to take into account other than net cash flows, such as the erosion on the existing revenue stream, the impact on existing financing, and the risk involved in reaping the projected reward.

Chapter
16

Financing Expansion

When is it time to grow and where will the money come from to do that? We look at how to make a business case for growth.

Introduction

Every small-business owner contemplates expanding at one stage of operations or another. Once you have had proven success with your business model, it's natural to think about how much more profit you can make using your entrepreneurial skills. Expanding your business has the potential to provide you with some of the following:

- **Economies of scale.** You may be able to add customers and revenue without increasing or expanding your current resources.

- **Increased profile.** Becoming a larger business may give you more stature in the community and may attract larger customers.

It had been almost a year since Earth-Power opened its doors for business. Judith had come on board four months ago as the full-time office manager and she had set up office procedures to make sure that the business was organized.

Craig spent most of his time conferencing with new customers and had just landed a large house builder out of New Orleans. The builder would include EarthPower's solar water heating units in all of its new houses in the coming year. The contract would bring in an additional $375,000 above Earth-Power's original revenue estimates.

Late on a Tuesday afternoon, Craig was talking to Sun Source, one of EarthPower's solar panel suppliers. The owner of Sun Source, Jason Freed, wanted to retire and pass the business on to his son. He complained to Craig that his son had no interest in running the business and he would have to sell it to someone else.

Craig thought about the conversation long after he hung up the telephone. Sun Source provided Earth-Power with almost all of its solar panels for its custom installations. If Earth-Power bought out Sun Source, the profit that would otherwise be going to someone else would instead be staying in the pockets of Craig and his partner.

Craig presented the proposal at the next meeting of the board of directors. John Wendsley immediately recognized the benefits of the proposal.

"We'll be able to control the supply of panels," he said. "That will certainly help if we grow as quickly as our projections suggest for next year."

- **Increased sales.** These may potentially (but not always) lead to greater profits.
- **Decreased risk.** If you are concerned about being economically dependent on a few large customers, expansion can provide the diversity of clientele needed to mitigate that risk.
- **Greater personal fulfillment.** You know that your business model works and can not only support you, but can become even larger.

Some entrepreneurs dream night and day of expanding their business. Others may be happy to grow their business to a certain size and then hold the fort, balancing work and other lifestyle issues. The decision to expand is based upon both financial and non-financial considerations.

Let's first have a look at the different types of expansion that you might contemplate.

Horizontal Expansion

Horizontal expansion means increasing your revenues from the same type of business as you are already in. There are five main ways to expand horizontally.

Increase your capacity

You can add new equipment, either more of the same type of equipment as you already have or new technology that will perform the same function less expensively and more efficiently. Increasing capacity would also include adding more staff to be able to handle higher sales volumes or renting or buying new office or warehouse space.

Expand your geographic area

You might choose to sell your products or services farther afield, either with a sales force, new bricks and mortar locations, or via the internet. You may also consider translating your packaging and advertising to be able to service foreign markets.

Develop new products or services

You may choose to increase your revenues by adding new products or services to your offerings. These products and services can be marketed to your existing customer base or to new markets.

This is usually referred to as "up selling." For a more in-depth discussion on up selling, you may wish to refer to the third book in the *Numbers 101 for Small Business* series, *Managing Business Growth*. Another reason to add new products or services is to more evenly spread out revenues, and thereby profits, throughout the year. For example, if you are a lawn-care company that generates most profits during the spring, summer, and fall months, you may consider adding snow plowing to your complement of services in order to generate profits in what would otherwise be the off season.

Develop a franchise

Once you have developed your business model and internal hard and soft systems, you may want to sell your business plans and systems to others who want to become small-business owners but who need guidance. If you choose this route, you would have two main revenue streams: profits from your own business and revenues from selling franchises.

Find new markets for your existing products and services

You may find that your product or service may have wider applications than those for which you originally planned. A great example of this is the Hummer. You've probably seen one: an oversized off-road vehicle that was originally developed for military applications. The Hummer has found its way into consumer use and now bears the mark of prestige for people with enough disposable income to purchase one. Finding new markets for existing products or services can be one of the lowest cost methods of expanding your business.

Vertical Expansion

Vertical expansion refers to reaping benefits from closely related operations. For example, if you own a delicatessen, it may make sense for you to purchase the cheese-making operation that sells you your cheese. That way, you can keep the profits that would otherwise be going to the cheese maker. Another example would be if your company designs electronic circuitry for use in consumer electronics, such as stereos and DVD players. You may consider producing the consumer products yourself and selling them through your own retail outlet, and thereby harvesting the profits that the manufacturer and the retailer would normally keep.

CASE STUDY
continued

The following week, EarthPower presented its offer to Jason Freed, who accepted it after consulting with his lawyer and accountant. Jason was happy that his company was being purchased by people who had the same commitment to alternative energy as he did. Craig and his partner were happy that they were able to integrate a critical operation into their own company.

Vertical expansion can also provide you with more control over your sources of supply. If you control the supply chain, production scheduling becomes easier and purchasing opportunities can benefit the entire chain. The risk of vertical expansion is that you might step on the toes of your customers or suppliers. You will now be competing in their markets as well. You may find that a competitor may not be as willing to sell to you now that you are battling head to head for customers.

The Dangers of Expansion

Now that we've looked at the benefits of expanding your business, we need to look at the potential risks. Many of these risks mirror those that you faced when first starting up your business. The repercussions of business failure are greater, however, once you have established your business and have created a rapport with your customers. You have more at stake now and the risks of expansion should be carefully weighed against the potential rewards. Consider some of the risks discussed below.

Liquidity issues

Expansion usually requires additional financing to purchase equipment, hire new staff, or develop new products. This increase in debt-servicing costs (that is to say, principal and interest payments) can stretch the business's resources thin, especially in the period directly following the expansion and before the increase in revenues happens. Proper cash flow planning and forecasting can go a long way towards making sure that you don't end up on the wrong side of "stretched thin."

Triggering call provisions

When planning the financing of your expansion, be sure to review all existing debt and equity financing contracts to ensure that you will not violate any of the provisions in them. For example, your existing bank loan contract may stipulate that you have a debt to equity ratio of no more than 1:1. If your new financing causes you to go over this limit, you run the risk of your bank calling the existing loan and you may find yourself scrambling to replace it. (See Table 1 in Chapter 7 for more detail on ratios.)

If you have equity investors, either in the form of minority shareholders or venture capitalists, make sure that you fully review the voting provisions in the agreements with regards to major decisions such as expansion and mergers and acquisitions.

Increase in fixed costs

If your expansion includes new fixed costs, such as equipment lease contracts or premises rental, your business is at a greater risk of loss if the new revenue streams do not occur as planned. For example, if your expansion plan calls for $75,000 in additional revenues in the first six months following the expansion, and the actual figures are only $50,000, you still must incur all of the additional fixed costs and this can put a strain on your existing operations. Careful cash flow forecasting and a backup financing plan can soften this risk.

Calculating the Benefits of Expansion

How do you know whether expanding your business makes financial sense? The decision process is much the same as the one you followed for starting your business in the first place. When you first made the decision about whether to buy an existing business or build one from scratch, you compared all of the inflows of cash from each business to the outflows. In a comparative situation like that, you would choose the one with the largest net cash inflow using the discounted cash flow method.

In deciding whether or not to expand, we use a similar process. In this situation, we will only need to look at the *changes* in cash flows from the expansion. Any cash flows that will be the same whether or not we expand will be ignored as they will have no bearing on our decision. We will also use the discounted cash flow method but this time, our decision will be based on whether there is a net inflow or outflow of cash over a period of time. If the cash flow is positive, it makes financial sense to expand. If it is negative, it does not.

Let's look at an example:

Grace owns a market garden operation. She farms three acres and grows a variety of organic vegetables, which she sells to area restaurants as well as at the local farmer's market on Saturday mornings. She is considering expanding her business to sell to more retail customers by delivering baskets of organic vegetables to their doors on a weekly basis for 17 weeks of the year. The baskets would be a mixture of the vegetables in season that week. Grace has estimated the following:

Costs:

- She will need to till an additional acre to service her estimated 125 new customers.

- Her operating costs (seeds, labor, equipment maintenance, fertilizer) for each acre average $9,410 per season.

- She will also need to acquire a van for deliveries and hire a delivery person for 35 hours per week at $12.50 per hour. The van costs will average $0.74 per mile and she estimates the mileage per season to be approximately 3,795 miles. The lease cost for the van will be $495 per month for 48 months (four years).

Revenues:

- Grace will charge each customer $425 per season for the basket program. This will be paid at the beginning of the season.

- She is expecting 50 customers in the first year and 70, 110, and 125 customers in years two, three, and four, respectively.

- She does not feel that the new program will cut into her farmer's market revenues at all.

Because Grace's fixed costs of the new venture, namely the lease payments on the van, extend over four years, we will look at the revenues and expenses over that period of time.

Table 3 shows the cash flows. The cash flows show that in the first year of operation, there is an expected loss on the basket program. Years two to four show net cash inflows. As we have seen earlier in this book, cash today is worth more than cash tomorrow. Therefore, early losses count for more than cash inflows later. In order to see if cash later is worth more or less than the earlier loss, we will use the discounted cash flow method to bring all of the net cash flows back to today. We will use the Present Value of $1 table in Appendix 1. Grace will have to finance the net cash outflow in year one with an operating line of credit from her bank that carries an interest rate of 12 percent, so we will use that rate for our discounting.

As you can see in Table 4, the net discounted cash flow attributed to the proposed expansion is positive, so it makes financial sense for Grace to go ahead. She will need to keep in mind that for

TABLE 3
CASH FLOWS FOR GRACE'S MARKET GARDEN

	1	2	3	4
Revenue	21,250	29,750	46,750	53,125
Acreage	9,410	9,410	9,410	9,410
Vehicle	2,808	2,808	2,808	2,808
Lease	5,940	5,940	5,940	5,940
Delivery	7,438	7,438	7,438	7,438
Loan interest	522	-	-	-
Net cash flow	**(4,868)**	**4,154**	**21,154**	**27,529**

the first season, she will have to finance the proposed cash short-fall, so this will need to be taken into account as she plans for the expansion.

Finding the Money to Expand

Once your business has a proven track record of financial success, your financing options begin to widen. Those who seemed reticent to lend to you when you were just starting out may be warming up to the investment possibilities as you plan your expansion.

Before you seek financing for the new operations, spend time updating your business plan, refining your cash flow forecasts, and honing your verbal presentation to potential investors or lenders. You are once again presenting yourself and your business and asking people to take a chance on you and give you money. You should be as professional as possible. You are now coming to the table as a seasoned entrepreneur, not just someone with a potentially good idea.

TABLE 4
DISCOUNTED CASH FLOWS FOR GRACE'S MARKET GARDEN

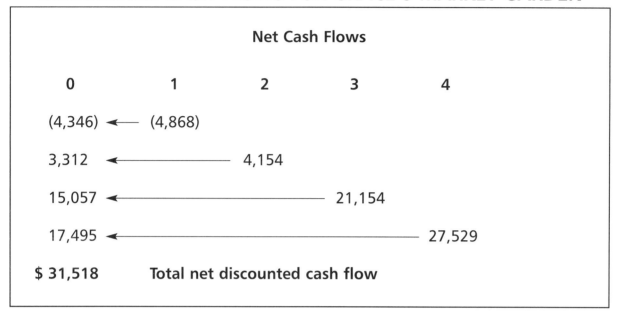

Net Cash Flows

0	1	2	3	4
(4,346) ◄— (4,868)				
3,312 ◄——— 4,154				
15,057 ◄———————— 21,154				
17,495 ◄———————————————— 27,529				

$ 31,518   **Total net discounted cash flow**

As you are updating your financial information, review your current financing structure. Are you getting the lowest interest rate possible on your borrowings? You may wish to refinance your current operations while you are seeking new financing. Start by talking to your bank. They may be more willing to renegotiate funding positions now that you have a track record.

Venture capitalists may also begin to show interest in your operations. Venture capitalists rarely lend money to start-ups but are more interested in the expansion of successful businesses. If your ultimate goal is to cash out of the business in five to ten years, this might be an avenue worth pursuing. For a more in-depth discussion of sources of financing, please refer to Chapters 7 and 8 regarding debt and equity financing, respectively.

Another source of financing available to you that wasn't when you first started up is internal cash flow. You may be able to divert profits from the current operations to fund the expansion in the short term. If you have significant equity investors, however, they may not be crazy about the idea of deferring the cash that should be in their pockets now for a potential slice of a bigger pie later. It's important to make sure that all lenders and investors are on board with your plans for expansion.

Chapter Summary

➡ Planning for the expansion of your business is much like the initial planning you undertook when you started up.

➡ You can expand horizontally, increasing your revenues by introducing new products or services or new markets, or you can expand vertically, increasing revenues by taking over connected operations.

➡ You can calculate the benefits of expansion by discounting the projected cash flows.

➡ There are more avenues of funding when you expand now that you have a proven financial track record.

Present Value of $1

PRESENT VALUE OF $1

PV TABLE

Discount Rate Period	1%	2%	3%	4%	5%	6%	7%	8%	9%	10%	12%	14%	16%	18%	20%	25%
1	0.9901	0.9804	0.9709	0.9615	0.9524	0.9434	0.9346	0.9259	0.9174	0.9091	0.8929	0.8772	0.8621	0.8475	0.8333	0.8000
2	0.9803	0.9612	0.9426	0.9246	0.9070	0.8900	0.8734	0.8573	0.8417	0.8264	0.7972	0.7695	0.7432	0.7182	0.6944	0.6400
3	0.9706	0.9423	0.9151	0.8890	0.8638	0.8396	0.8163	0.7938	0.7722	0.7513	0.7118	0.6750	0.6407	0.6086	0.5787	0.5120
4	0.9610	0.9238	0.8885	0.8548	0.8227	0.7921	0.7629	0.7350	0.7084	0.6830	0.6355	0.5921	0.5523	0.5158	0.4823	0.4096
5	0.9515	0.9057	0.8626	0.8219	0.7835	0.7473	0.7130	0.6806	0.6499	0.6209	0.5674	0.5194	0.4761	0.4371	0.4019	0.3277
6	0.9420	0.8880	0.8375	0.7903	0.7462	0.7050	0.6663	0.6302	0.5963	0.5645	0.5066	0.4556	0.4104	0.3704	0.3349	0.2621
7	0.9327	0.8706	0.8131	0.7599	0.7107	0.6651	0.6227	0.5835	0.5470	0.5132	0.4523	0.3996	0.3538	0.3139	0.2791	0.2097
8	0.9235	0.8535	0.7894	0.7307	0.6768	0.6274	0.5820	0.5403	0.5019	0.4665	0.4039	0.3506	0.3050	0.2660	0.2326	0.1678
9	0.9143	0.8368	0.7664	0.7026	0.6446	0.5919	0.5439	0.5002	0.4604	0.4241	0.3606	0.3075	0.2630	0.2255	0.1938	0.1342
10	0.9053	0.8203	0.7441	0.6756	0.6139	0.5584	0.5083	0.4632	0.4224	0.3855	0.3220	0.2697	0.2267	0.1911	0.1615	0.1074
11	0.8963	0.8043	0.7224	0.6496	0.5847	0.5268	0.4751	0.4289	0.3875	0.3505	0.2875	0.2366	0.1954	0.1619	0.1346	0.0859
12	0.8874	0.7885	0.7014	0.6246	0.5568	0.4970	0.4440	0.3971	0.3555	0.3186	0.2567	0.2076	0.1685	0.1372	0.1122	0.0687
13	0.8787	0.7730	0.6810	0.6006	0.5303	0.4688	0.4150	0.3677	0.3262	0.2897	0.2292	0.1821	0.1452	0.1163	0.0935	0.0550
14	0.8700	0.7579	0.6611	0.5775	0.5051	0.4423	0.3878	0.3405	0.2992	0.2633	0.2046	0.1597	0.1252	0.0985	0.0779	0.0440
15	0.8613	0.7430	0.6419	0.5553	0.4810	0.4173	0.3624	0.3152	0.2745	0.2394	0.1827	0.1401	0.1079	0.0835	0.0649	0.0352
16	0.8528	0.7284	0.6232	0.5339	0.4581	0.3936	0.3387	0.2919	0.2519	0.2176	0.1631	0.1229	0.0930	0.0708	0.0541	0.0281
17	0.8444	0.7142	0.6050	0.5134	0.4363	0.3714	0.3166	0.2703	0.2311	0.1978	0.1456	0.1078	0.0802	0.0600	0.0451	0.0225
18	0.8360	0.7002	0.5874	0.4936	0.4155	0.3503	0.2959	0.2502	0.2120	0.1799	0.1300	0.0946	0.0691	0.0508	0.0376	0.0180
19	0.8277	0.6864	0.5703	0.4746	0.3957	0.3305	0.2765	0.2317	0.1945	0.1635	0.1161	0.0829	0.0596	0.0431	0.0313	0.0144
20	0.8195	0.6730	0.5537	0.4564	0.3769	0.3118	0.2584	0.2145	0.1784	0.1486	0.1037	0.0728	0.0514	0.0365	0.0261	0.0115
21	0.8114	0.6598	0.5375	0.4388	0.3589	0.2942	0.2415	0.1987	0.1637	0.1351	0.0926	0.0638	0.0443	0.0309	0.0217	0.0092
22	0.8034	0.6468	0.5219	0.4220	0.3418	0.2775	0.2257	0.1839	0.1502	0.1228	0.0826	0.0560	0.0382	0.0262	0.0181	0.0074
23	0.7954	0.6342	0.5067	0.4057	0.3256	0.2618	0.2109	0.1703	0.1378	0.1117	0.0738	0.0491	0.0329	0.0222	0.0151	0.0059
24	0.7876	0.6217	0.4919	0.3901	0.3101	0.2470	0.1971	0.1577	0.1264	0.1015	0.0659	0.0431	0.0284	0.0188	0.0126	0.0047

Present Value of
an Annuity

Period, n	Discount Rate, k																			
	1%	2%	3%	4%	5%	6%	7%	8%	9%	10%	11%	12%	13%	14%	15%	16%	17%	18%	19%	20%
1	0.990	0.980	0.971	0.962	0.952	0.943	0.935	0.926	0.917	0.909	0.901	0.893	0.885	0.877	0.870	0.862	0.855	0.847	0.840	0.833
2	1.970	1.942	1.913	1.886	1.859	1.833	1.808	1.783	1.759	1.736	1.713	1.690	1.668	1.647	1.626	1.605	1.585	1.566	1.547	1.528
3	2.941	2.884	2.829	2.775	2.723	2.673	2.624	2.577	2.531	2.487	2.444	2.402	2.361	2.322	2.283	2.246	2.210	2.174	2.140	2.106
4	3.902	3.808	3.717	3.630	3.546	3.465	3.387	3.312	3.240	3.170	3.102	3.037	2.974	2.914	2.855	2.798	2.743	2.690	2.639	2.589
5	4.853	4.713	4.580	4.452	4.329	4.212	4.100	3.993	3.890	3.791	3.696	3.605	3.517	3.433	3.352	3.274	3.199	3.127	3.058	2.991
6	5.795	5.601	5.417	5.242	5.076	4.917	4.767	4.623	4.486	4.355	4.231	4.111	3.998	3.889	3.784	3.685	3.589	3.498	3.410	3.326
7	6.728	6.472	6.230	6.002	5.786	5.582	5.389	5.206	5.033	4.868	4.712	4.564	4.423	4.288	4.160	4.039	3.922	3.812	3.706	3.605
8	7.652	7.325	7.020	6.733	6.463	6.210	5.971	5.747	5.535	5.335	5.146	4.968	4.799	4.639	4.487	4.344	4.207	4.078	3.954	3.837
9	8.566	8.162	7.786	7.435	7.108	6.802	6.515	6.247	5.995	5.759	5.537	5.328	5.132	4.946	4.772	4.607	4.451	4.303	4.163	4.031
10	9.471	8.983	8.530	8.111	7.722	7.360	7.024	6.710	6.418	6.145	5.889	5.650	5.426	5.216	5.019	4.833	4.659	4.494	4.339	4.192
11	10.368	9.787	9.253	8.760	8.306	7.887	7.499	7.139	6.805	6.495	6.207	5.938	5.687	5.453	5.234	5.029	4.836	4.656	4.486	4.327
12	11.255	10.575	9.954	9.385	8.863	8.384	7.943	7.536	7.161	6.814	6.492	6.194	5.918	5.660	5.421	5.197	4.988	4.793	4.611	4.439
13	12.134	11.348	10.635	9.986	9.394	8.853	8.358	7.904	7.487	7.103	6.750	6.424	6.122	5.842	5.583	5.342	5.118	4.910	4.715	4.533
14	13.004	12.106	11.296	10.563	9.899	9.295	8.745	8.244	7.786	7.367	6.982	6.628	6.302	6.002	5.724	5.468	5.229	5.008	4.802	4.611
15	13.865	12.849	11.938	11.118	10.380	9.712	9.108	8.559	8.061	7.606	7.191	6.811	6.462	6.142	5.847	5.575	5.324	5.092	4.876	4.675
16	14.718	13.578	12.561	11.652	10.838	10.106	9.447	8.851	8.313	7.824	7.379	6.974	6.604	6.265	5.954	5.668	5.405	5.162	4.938	4.730
17	15.562	14.292	13.166	12.166	11.274	10.477	9.763	9.122	8.544	8.022	7.549	7.120	6.729	6.373	6.047	5.749	5.475	5.222	4.990	4.775
18	16.398	14.992	13.754	12.659	11.690	10.828	10.059	9.372	8.756	8.201	7.702	7.250	6.840	6.467	6.128	5.818	5.534	5.273	5.033	4.812
19	17.226	15.678	14.324	13.134	12.085	11.158	10.336	9.604	8.950	8.365	7.839	7.366	6.938	6.550	6.198	5.877	5.584	5.316	5.070	4.843
20	18.046	16.351	14.877	13.590	12.462	11.470	10.594	9.818	9.129	8.514	7.963	7.469	7.025	6.623	6.259	5.929	5.628	5.353	5.101	4.870
21	18.857	17.011	15.415	14.029	12.821	11.764	10.836	10.017	9.292	8.649	8.075	7.562	7.102	6.687	6.312	5.973	5.665	5.384	5.127	4.891
22	19.660	17.658	15.937	14.451	13.163	12.042	11.061	10.201	9.442	8.772	8.176	7.645	7.170	6.743	6.359	6.011	5.696	5.410	5.149	4.909
23	20.456	18.292	16.444	14.857	13.489	12.303	11.272	10.371	9.580	8.883	8.266	7.718	7.230	6.792	6.399	6.044	5.723	5.432	5.167	4.925
24	21.243	18.914	16.936	15.247	13.799	12.550	11.469	10.529	9.707	8.985	8.348	7.784	7.283	6.835	6.434	6.073	5.746	5.451	5.182	4.937
25	22.023	19.523	17.413	15.622	14.094	12.783	11.654	10.675	9.823	9.077	8.422	7.843	7.330	6.873	6.464	6.097	5.766	5.467	5.195	4.948
26	22.795	20.121	17.877	15.983	14.375	13.003	11.826	10.810	9.929	9.161	8.488	7.896	7.372	6.906	6.491	6.118	5.783	5.480	5.206	4.956
27	23.560	20.707	18.327	16.330	14.643	13.211	11.987	10.935	10.027	9.237	8.548	7.943	7.409	6.935	6.514	6.136	5.798	5.492	5.215	4.964
28	24.316	21.281	18.764	16.663	14.898	13.406	12.137	11.051	10.116	9.307	8.602	7.984	7.441	6.961	6.534	6.152	5.810	5.502	5.223	4.970
29	25.066	21.844	19.188	16.984	15.141	13.591	12.278	11.158	10.198	9.370	8.650	8.022	7.470	6.983	6.551	6.166	5.820	5.510	5.229	4.975
30	25.808	22.396	19.600	17.292	15.372	13.765	12.409	11.258	10.274	9.427	8.694	8.055	7.496	7.003	6.566	6.177	5.829	5.517	5.235	4.979
35	29.409	24.999	21.487	18.665	16.374	14.498	12.948	11.655	10.567	9.644	8.855	8.176	7.586	7.070	6.617	6.215	5.858	5.539	5.251	4.992
40	32.835	27.355	23.115	19.793	17.159	15.046	13.332	11.925	10.757	9.779	8.951	8.244	7.634	7.105	6.642	6.233	5.871	5.548	5.258	4.997
45	36.095	29.490	24.519	20.720	17.774	15.456	13.606	12.108	10.881	9.863	9.008	8.283	7.661	7.123	6.654	6.242	5.877	5.552	5.261	4.999
50	39.196	31.424	25.730	21.482	18.256	15.762	13.801	12.233	10.962	9.915	9.042	8.304	7.675	7.133	6.661	6.246	5.880	5.554	5.262	4.999

Future Value of
an Annuity

FUTURE VALUE OF AN ANNUITY

Period, n	Compound Rate, k																			
	1%	2%	3%	4%	5%	6%	7%	8%	9%	10%	11%	12%	13%	14%	15%	16%	17%	18%	19%	20%
1	1.000	1.000	1.000	1.000	1.000	1.000	1.000	1.000	1.000	1.000	1.000	1.000	1.000	1.000	1.000	1.000	1.000	1.000	1.000	1.000
2	2.010	2.020	2.030	2.040	2.050	2.060	2.070	2.080	2.090	2.100	2.110	2.120	2.130	2.140	2.150	2.160	2.170	2.180	2.190	2.200
3	3.030	3.060	3.091	3.122	3.152	3.184	3.215	3.246	3.278	3.310	3.342	3.374	3.407	3.440	3.473	3.506	3.539	3.572	3.606	3.640
4	4.060	4.122	4.184	4.246	4.310	4.375	4.440	4.506	4.573	4.641	4.710	4.779	4.850	4.921	4.993	5.066	5.141	5.215	5.291	5.368
5	5.101	5.204	5.309	5.416	5.526	5.637	5.751	5.867	5.985	6.105	6.228	6.353	6.480	6.610	6.742	6.877	7.014	7.154	7.297	7.442
6	6.152	6.308	6.468	6.633	6.802	6.975	7.153	7.336	7.523	7.716	7.913	8.115	8.323	8.536	8.754	8.977	9.207	9.442	9.683	9.930
7	7.214	7.434	7.662	7.898	8.142	8.394	8.654	8.923	9.200	9.487	9.783	10.089	10.405	10.730	11.067	11.414	11.772	12.142	12.523	12.916
8	8.286	8.583	8.892	9.214	9.549	9.897	10.260	10.637	11.028	11.436	11.859	12.300	12.757	13.233	13.727	14.240	14.773	15.327	15.902	16.499
9	9.369	9.755	10.159	10.583	11.027	11.491	11.978	12.488	13.021	13.579	14.164	14.776	15.416	16.085	16.786	17.519	18.285	19.086	19.923	20.799
10	10.462	10.950	11.464	12.006	12.578	13.181	13.816	14.487	15.193	15.937	16.722	17.549	18.420	19.337	20.304	21.321	22.393	23.521	24.709	25.959
11	11.567	12.169	12.808	13.486	14.207	14.972	15.784	16.645	17.560	18.531	19.561	20.655	21.814	23.045	24.349	25.733	27.200	28.755	30.404	32.150
12	12.683	13.412	14.192	15.026	15.917	16.870	17.888	18.977	20.141	21.384	22.713	24.133	25.650	27.271	29.002	30.850	32.824	34.931	37.180	39.581
13	13.809	14.680	15.618	16.627	17.713	18.882	20.141	21.495	22.953	24.523	26.212	28.029	29.985	32.089	34.352	36.786	39.404	42.219	45.244	48.497
14	14.947	15.974	17.086	18.292	19.599	21.015	22.550	24.215	26.019	27.975	30.095	32.393	34.883	37.581	40.505	43.672	47.103	50.818	54.841	59.196
15	16.097	17.293	18.599	20.024	21.579	23.276	25.129	27.152	29.361	31.772	34.405	37.280	40.417	43.842	47.580	51.660	56.110	60.965	66.261	72.035
16	17.258	18.639	20.157	21.825	23.657	25.673	27.888	30.324	33.003	35.950	39.190	42.753	46.672	50.980	55.717	60.925	66.649	72.939	79.850	87.442
17	18.430	20.012	21.762	23.698	25.840	28.213	30.840	33.750	36.974	40.545	44.501	48.884	53.739	59.118	65.075	71.673	78.979	87.068	96.022	105.93
18	19.615	21.412	23.414	25.645	28.132	30.906	33.999	37.450	41.301	45.599	50.396	55.750	61.725	68.394	75.836	84.141	93.406	103.74	115.27	128.12
19	20.811	22.841	25.117	27.671	30.539	33.760	37.379	41.446	46.018	51.159	56.939	63.440	70.749	78.969	88.212	98.603	110.28	123.41	138.17	154.74
20	22.019	24.297	26.870	29.778	33.066	36.786	40.996	45.762	51.160	57.275	64.203	72.052	80.947	91.025	102.44	115.38	130.03	146.63	165.42	186.69
21	23.239	25.783	28.676	31.969	35.719	39.993	44.865	50.423	56.765	64.002	72.265	81.699	92.470	104.77	118.81	134.84	153.14	174.02	197.85	225.03
22	24.472	27.299	30.537	34.248	38.505	43.392	49.006	55.457	62.873	71.403	81.214	92.503	105.49	120.44	137.63	157.41	180.17	206.34	236.44	271.03
23	25.716	28.845	32.453	36.618	41.430	46.996	53.436	60.893	69.532	79.543	91.148	104.60	120.20	138.30	159.28	183.60	211.80	244.49	282.36	326.24
24	26.973	30.422	34.426	39.083	44.502	50.816	58.177	66.765	76.790	88.497	102.17	118.16	136.83	158.66	184.17	213.98	248.81	289.49	337.01	392.48
25	28.243	32.030	36.459	41.646	47.727	54.865	63.249	73.106	84.701	98.347	114.41	133.33	155.62	181.87	212.79	249.21	292.10	342.60	402.04	471.98
26	29.526	33.671	38.553	44.312	51.113	59.156	68.676	79.954	93.324	109.18	128.00	150.33	176.85	208.33	245.71	290.09	342.76	405.27	479.43	567.38
27	30.821	35.344	40.710	47.084	54.669	63.706	74.484	87.351	102.72	121.10	143.08	169.37	200.84	238.50	283.57	337.50	402.03	479.22	571.52	681.85
28	32.129	37.051	42.931	49.968	58.403	68.528	80.698	95.339	112.97	134.21	159.82	190.70	227.95	272.89	327.10	392.50	471.38	566.48	681.11	819.22
29	33.450	38.792	45.219	52.966	62.323	73.640	87.347	103.97	124.14	148.63	178.40	214.58	258.58	312.09	377.17	456.30	552.51	669.45	811.52	984.07
30	34.785	40.568	47.575	56.085	66.439	79.058	94.461	113.28	136.31	164.49	199.02	241.33	293.20	356.79	434.75	530.31	647.44	790.95	966.71	1181.9
35	41.660	49.994	60.462	73.652	90.320	111.43	138.24	172.32	215.71	271.02	341.59	431.66	546.68	693.57	881.17	1120.7	1426.5	1816.7	2314.2	2948.3
40	48.886	60.402	75.401	95.026	120.80	154.76	199.64	259.06	337.88	442.59	581.83	767.09	1013.7	1342.0	1779.1	2360.8	3134.5	4163.2	5529.8	7343.9
45	56.481	71.893	92.720	121.03	159.70	212.74	285.75	386.51	525.86	718.90	986.64	1358.2	1874.2	2590.6	3585.1	4965.3	6879.3	9531.6	13203	18281
50	64.463	84.579	112.80	152.67	209.35	290.34	406.53	573.77	815.08	1163.9	1668.8	2400.0	3459.5	4994.5	7217.7	10435	15089	21813	31515	45497

Resources for the Growing Business

Online Resources

www.numbers101.com

Our official website is packed full of articles, advice, and business tools such as cashflow spreadsheets, templates and links. You can also sign up for our free newsletter and join our online Numbers 101 community, linking small businesses all over the world!

www.self-counsel.com

Online shopping for a wide variety of business and legal titles (including this one and other titles in the *Numbers 101 for Small Business* series).

www.sba.gov

US Small Business Administration — lots of great resources for small businesses. Mostly US focused but useful for companies in all countries.

www.cfib.ca

Canadian Federation of Independent Business. CFIB is an advocacy group for small businesses. They lobby the government for legislative changes that will assist businesses and their owners. On the website are lease-versus-buy calculators, downloadable publications, and other resources.

http://sme.ic.gc.ca

Performance Plus from Industry Canada. A great website for businesses from all countries. Shows you how your business stacks up with others in your industry.

www.bcentral.com

Microsoft Small Business Resources. Do they want to sell you stuff? Of course! In addition, this website also offers great articles on marketing, promotion, and other business matters.

www.toolkit.cch.com

CCH Business Owner's Toolkit. Great tools and resources, including sample business documents, checklists, and government forms.

www.inc.com

The online presence of *Inc.* magazine. Here you will find great articles, tools, and calculators to help your business grow.

Must-Read Books for Entrepreneurs

Building a Shared Vision: A Leader's Guide to Aligning the Organization by C. Patrick Lewis (Oregon: Productivity Press, 1997)

This book helps you to bring your vision down to the organization level.

Good to Great: Why Some Companies Make the Leap and Others Don't by Jim Collins (New York: Harper Business, 2001)

Whether you have one employee or thousands, this book will show you how great leaders make great companies.

Inside the Magic Kingdom: Seven Keys to Disney's Success by Tom Connellan (Bard Press, 1997).

A look at one of the most successful team-oriented companies in the world.

From Worst to First: Behind the Scenes of Continental's Remarkable Comeback by Gordon Bethune (Wiley, 1999).

This book follows Continental's meteoric rise in three years from its mediocre beginnings. A great case study on how strong leadership can make fantastic changes in an organization.

Pour Your Heart Into It: How Starbucks Built a Company One Cup at a Time by Howard Schultz (Hyperion, 1999).

Starbucks began with the vision of its CEO and the author of this book, Howard Schultz. He has turned it into a marketing phenomenon and one of the fastest growing companies in the world.

Body and Soul by Anita Roddick (Crown Publishing, 1991).

When Roddick started The Body Shop, she had a very different vision in mind than most entrepreneurs. She shows us that it is possible to succeed by marching to the beat of your own drummer!

The Nordstrom Way: The Inside Story of America's #1 Customer Service Company by Robert Spector & Patrick D. McCarthy (Wiley, 1996).

Customer service can make or break a company. Learn how Nordstrom has made rabidly loyal customers and how you can too.

McDonald's: Behind the Arches by John F. Love (Bantam, 1995).

An inside look at the most successful franchise on the planet.

Virgin King: Inside Richard Branson's Business Empire by Tim Jackson (HarperCollins, 1998).

Richard Branson is one of the most individual and successful entrepreneurs in the world. Learn how he took Virgin Airlines from its humble beginnings to become one of the most-loved and profitable underdogs.

Nuts! Southwest Airlines' Crazy Recipe for Business and Personal Success by Kevin Freiberg and Jackie Freiberg (Broadway Books, 1998).

There is no other business model quite like Southwest Airlines'. They have truly listened to their customers and have developed fantastic systems to help them meet their goals. A great book on systemization and an in-depth look at a fascinating company.

Glossary

Annuity: A series of constant or level cash flows that occurs at the end of each period for a fixed number of periods.

Balance sheet: One of the three major financial statements of a business. (The statement of cash flow and the income statement are the other two.) The balance sheet displays everything of a measurable financial value that is owned and owed by the company.

Budgeting: The process of planning and projecting revenues, expenses, and capital expenditures for future fiscal periods.

Business risk: The total amount of danger of loss a business faces from both internal and external factors, such as competition, foreign exchange rate changes, inadequate internal management, and market concentration.

Capacity: The upper limit of a business's ability to produce a product or service.

Capital: The resources that a business uses to produce a product or service.

Cash flow: The inflows to and outflows from a business, regardless of the source.

Cash flow statement (also known as the statement of changes in financial position or the statement of cash flows): One of the three major financial statements of a business. (The balance sheet and income statement are the other two.) The cash flow statement, in its most general terms, shows why there is an increase or decrease in cash during the year.

Controller (comptroller): The "big cheese" accountant in an organization. The controller oversees all accounting functions and sometimes operates as the company's chief financial officer.

Conversion rate: The number of potential customers who buy versus the number who inquire about your product or service.

Corporation: One of the three major forms of business ownership (partnership and sole proprietorship are the other two.) A corporation is the only type of business that is legally separate from its owners: it is itself a legal entity. Corporate ownership is shown through the issues of share certificates.

Creditor: A person or other business that has loaned money or extended credit to a business.

Debt: The amounts owed by a business to outside persons or businesses. It is sometimes more narrowly defined as to exclude accounts payable and include only loans that have fixed interest rates and repayment schedules.

Debt financing: The amount of capital raised by a business through borrowing. Sources of debt financing include banks, trust companies, credit cards, and leasing companies.

Decline: The last of three stages in a company's life cycle, in which revenues and customer base begin to decline. The other two are infancy and maturity.

Demand: The desire by consumers for a business's product.

Dividends: The portion of earnings (either current or retained from prior periods) that have been distributed out to the shareholders in the current operating period.

Dun & Bradstreet: A corporate rating agency in the United States.

Earnings: A term usually used interchangeably with net income (i.e., revenues less expenses).

Entrepreneur: A person who envisions and creates a business. This person may or may not be either an investor or manager in the ongoing operations.

Equity: The total amount of recoverable capital the owners of a business have invested.

Equity financing: The amount of capital raised through the sale of partial ownership in a business.

Exit strategy: A plan for a business's owners to either sell or wind up the business.

Franchise: A company that designs and builds a business model for entrepreneurs to follow.

General ledger: The grouping of accounts used by a business. Also, the book where the main summary records are kept for each balance sheet and income statement item.

General journal: A detailed record of all financial transactions of a business. The general journal is summarized and entered as net increases and decreases to the accounts in the general ledger.

Goodwill: The value of a business that is not directly attributable to hard assets but instead to the benefits such as a business's reputation or customer list.

Gross income: Another term for revenues.

Gross margin: Represents revenues minus the cost of goods sold in the period.

Income statement: One of the three major financial statements of a business. (The balance sheet and statement of cash flow are the other two.) The income statement shows operating activity over an operating period from revenues, expenses, and extraordinary gains and losses.

Hard systems: Those business systems that involve tangible procedures, for example, how a management report is prepared.

Infancy: The first of three stages in a company's life cycle, in which revenues increase exponentially and cash flow is generally strained. The other two are maturity and decline.

Insolvent: A term used to describe a business that does not have enough assets to meet its debt obligations in the short term. Insolvency can lead to bankruptcy if not corrected quickly.

Internal control: Represents the procedures set up in a business to prevent errors and fraudulent activity.

Inventory: Goods held for resale that remain unsold at the end of an operating period. In a manufacturing environment, inventory includes raw materials, goods in the process of being made, and finished goods. In certain service industries, inventory includes time spent on customer activities but not yet billed out.

Life cycle of a business: Represents the three stages of the total existence of a business: infancy, maturity, and decline.

Management operational plan: A company's plan for how it will do business on a day-to-day basis. A management operational plan will include short-term budgets and revenue forecasts as well as analysis of historical performance (see the second book in the *Numbers 101 for Small Business* series, *Financial Management 101*, for a more complete discussion of the management operational plan).

Manager: The individual that oversees the production staff and ensures that policies and procedures are being followed.

Market niche: The specific set of consumer demands that are met by a business.

Market share: The number of customers a business has as compared to all of the customers for that particular product or service.

Maturity: The second of three stages in a company's life cycle, in which revenues and customer base are steady and customer demand has been sated. The other two are infancy and decline.

Mission statement: A company's representation of its vision and how it will achieve it.

Net income: The income left in an accounting period after all expenses have been deducted from revenues. The term net income is used only if the revenues exceed the expenses.

Net loss: The deficit for an accounting period that occurs when the expenses for that period exceed the revenues.

Partnership: One of the three major forms of business ownership. (corporation and sole proprietor are the other two.) A partnership is an unincorporated business with two or more owners. Partnerships are jointly owned by the partners and do not have a separate "legal life" of their own.

Profit: see **Net income.**

Profit and loss (P&L) statement: Another name for an income statement.

Return on investment (ROI): The amount of investment income an investor makes on an investment divided by the amount invested.

Revenue: The amount of net assets generated by a business as a result of its operations.

Shareholder: An owner or internal investor of a corporation.

Soft systems: Those business systems that involve intangible procedures, more particularly, the actions of employees. For example, how a customer is greeted on the telephone or how a customer complaint is handled.

Sole proprietorship: One of the three major forms of business ownership. (Corporation and partnership are the other two.) A sole proprietorship is an unincorporated company owned by a single owner. It has no "legal life" of its own.

Solvency: The ability of a company to settle its liabilities with its assets.

Statement of cash flows: One of the three major financial statements. The statement of cash flow explains the changes in assets, liabilities, and net equity for the period.

Statement of changes in financial position: An older term for the statement of cash flows.

Stockholder: see **Shareholder.**

Systems: The group of business systems that make up the operations of a company.

Turnkey: A business that has had policies and procedures well-documented and tested so that anyone can run it successfully from the very beginning.

Vision statement: A company's overall statement as to how it views itself in the future. A vision statement is broken down further into a measurable mission statement and actionable operational goals.

If you found *Financing Your Business* useful, get *Managing Business Growth*, also available from Self-Counsel Press. Here's a preview of its table of contents:

Contents

Appendix 1 — Resources for the Growing Business

Online Resources

Must-Read Books for Entrepreneurs

Glossary

Diagrams

1 The Four Foundation Walls
2 The Life Cycle of a Business
3 Typical Time Chart for a Business Owner
4 Recommended Time Chart for a Business Owner

Samples

1 Customer Survey Form
2 Billings by Customer
3 Terminating a Customer
4 Vision Statements
5 Mission Statements
6 Telephone Interactions
7 Potential Customer Interaction Review
8 Telephone Script
9 Documenting Your Work Processes
10 Employment Advertisement
11 Human Resource Policy
12 Valuing a Business Acquisition

Checklists

1 The Successful Entrepreneur
2 The Life Cycle of a Business
3 A Systems Approach
4 Analyzing the Status Quo
5 Growing Your Business
6 Getting a Handle on Your Revenues
7 Your Strategy
8 Testing Change
9 Your Product or Service

FEB 2005

8/18